Iyashino Gendai Reiki Ho

A Modern Reiki Method for Healing

Revised Edition

癒しの
現代霊気法

Iyashino Gendai Reiki Ho

A Modern Reiki Method for Healing

Revised Edition

Hiroshi Doi
土居裕

Notice to Readers

The ability to channel Reiki energy cannot be learned by reading this book. This ability is opened in the student by a reiju (attunement) given by a Reiki Master during a Reiki class taken in person. This book will help potential students decide if they would like to take a Reiki class. And it is also valuable to those who have already taken a Reiki class.

The ideas and techniques described in this book are not meant as an independent guide for self-healing. If you have a health condition and intend to use Reiki, please do so under the supervision of an enlightened medical doctor or health care professional.

ISBN 1-886785-31-7

Library of Congress Control Number: 2013954262

Published in the United States of America.

Vision Publications
21421 Hilltop St. #28, Southfield, MI 48033
Phone (800) 332-8112, (248) 948-8112 Fax (248) 948-9534
E-mail center@reiki.org Web site www.reiki.org

Acknowledgements

The photo model for the basic 12
hand positions is Honoka Doi, 5 years old.

Editing
Rick Rivard, Miyuki Iwasaki,
Rosemary Pearson (Revised Edition),
William Lee Rand (Revised Edition)

Translation
Rick Rivard, Miyuki Iwasaki, Akiko Kawarai
Mari Marchand, Hiroko & Phillip Kelly,
Emiko Arai, Yukio Miura, Yuko Okamoto,
Fumi Koji (Revised Edition)

Book Layout and Cover
Corey Hogan Bippes

Table of Contents

Part III. Self-Purifying and Self-Growth Giho

About Gendai Reiki Ho

GENDAI REIKI HO DOES NOT TEACH the same exact system of Reiki as is taught by the Usui Reiki Ryoho Gakkai. Its purpose is to create a resonance between Reiki and it's use within the everyday life of our modern society. Gendai Reiki Ho's attunement methods have been developed based on Western Reiki, not on 霊授 the reiju of the Usui Reiki Ryoho Gakkai. The Gendai Reiki Ho attunement method is not the same as what was practiced by Usui Sensei. It is patterned after the Western style attunement because it has many aspects that are better suited to modern people since the physical constitution and lifestyle is different compared to that of Usui Sensei's time.

Foreword

SHORTLY AFTER BECOMING A REIKI MASTER, I realized that while the style of Reiki that was being taught in the West was effective, there were unusual problems with the history. Many of the important ideas in the history had proven to be more of an allegory than something based on factual information. It became clear that up to that point, no one in the West had done evidence-based research into the history of Reiki; instead the story that was being taught at the time had simply been accepted and passed on. I knew that in order to have a true understanding of the essence of Reiki, it was essential to have an accurate history and also to understand the character of Usui Sensei and what motivated him to meditate on Kurama Yama where he received this miraculous gift. I also knew that in solving this mystery, it was possible that we'd discover important information about the system of Reiki healing he developed that would help us be better healers.

I continued to look for authentic information about the history of Reiki and began making progress. In 1997, Arjava Petter published his first book, which contained the location of Usui Sensei's grave along with a translation of the inscription on the Usui memorial stone; in this same year, I made my first research trip to Japan. In 1999 I made a second trip to Japan to do research for *The Spirit of Reiki,* a book I was writing with Arjava Petter and Walter Lubeck. It was on this trip that I first met Doi Sensei in an arranged meeting in a restaurant in Kyoto. This was an exciting time for Reiki research as it was just before this, on May 13, 1998, that Doi Sensei had published the first edition of this book in Japan, and it was also close to the time when he taught his first class in the West, in Vancouver, British Columbia in August 1999.

Then in October 2002, I had the honor of taking his Gendai Reiki Ho Master Special Course in Toronto, Canada. Later I had the opportunity to conduct two interviews with Doi Sensei that appeared in the Summer and Fall 2003 issues of *Reiki News Magazine*. It is through these experiences that I have gotten to know Doi Sensei and therefore to appreciate the important contributions he has made to the practice of Reiki.

As a member of the Usui Reiki Ryoho Gakkai, Doi Sensei is in a unique position to offer authentic information about the history and practice of Reiki. The Gakkai was founded by Usui Sensei in April 1922 with the purpose of preserving and promoting his teachings. Usui Sensei was the first president and the following four presidents were all Shinpi-den who were trained by Usui

Sensei and were authorized by him to give reiju (attunements) and to teach with the same knowledge and authority as Usui Sensei as well as to teach in his place when he was not present.[1] Therefore, the information that is kept in Gakkai archives and the teachings the Gakkai provides to its members have the highest level of authenticity. Doi Sensei has access to this information and contact with current members including two of its recent presidents. He has made use of these resources along with his experience with Western Reiki in creating Gendai Reiki Ho and in writing this book.

Since its discovery and its introduction to the West, Reiki has grown in popularity. There are now millions of people the world over who love Reiki for the difference it makes in their lives. Reiki provides healing for every kind of physical illness or condition as well as for mental and emotional issues. It offers help for solving virtually any problem or difficulty. And as Usui Sensei said, it is a method for creating happiness. We can only marvel at the wonderful benefits it provides for so many people.

And so I encourage everyone who reads this book to do so with gratitude and appreciation for Usui Sensei, for the members of the Gakkai and for its author Doi Sensei, each of whom has taken responsibility to preserve the methods, the wisdom and especially the essence of this sacred practice.

William Lee Rand
September 2013

[1] An exception to this is Yoshiharu Wantanabe who recieved Oku-den Koki from Usui Sensei and was given Shinpi-den from Juzaburo Ushida after Usui Sensei passed.

A Message from Japan, Birthplace of Reiki For Readers of the English Version

IT IS A GREAT PLEASURE FOR ME that the revised translation of *Iyashi no Gendai Reiki Ho* is being published for Reiki practitioners abroad. When the Great Earthquake generated a tsunami, and the nuclear reactor was damaged on March 11, 2011, we received a lot of healing energy from all over the world. I truly hope I can convey our appreciation to all of you along with the contents of this book.

臼井霊気療法 (Usui Reiki Ryoho) is now practiced worldwide, but after World War II, the name of 'Reiki' appeared to be completely forgotten in Japan. Teachers and practitioners of the Western style of Reiki believed that Japanese Reiki had disappeared after Japan's defeat and that 臼井霊気療法学会 (the Usui Reiki Ryoho Gakkai), which was the Reiki association founded by 臼井先生 (Usui Sensei), did not exist anymore. The Reiki schools that brought Reiki into Japan again told us the same thing. And it was accepted without much question when the first Japanese edition of this book was published.

Reiki first came back to Japan through the Radiance Technique in the late 1980s. Although its teachers told me that the Japanese Reiki system was dissolved, I had hopes that there might still be some former members of the group even after the dissolution. I did all I could do to find them, but in vain. So I had to believe what I was told.

In July 1993, I went to a crystal healing seminar in Tokyo where I had a miracle encounter. I discovered that a lady (Ms. Uka Onoda, a Buddhist statue sculptor) who happened to be one of my healing partners at the seminar was a long-time member of the Usui Reiki Ryoho Gakkai. She told me that it was still alive and well and that its sixth president, Ms. Kimiko Koyama, was continuing its tradition. In October of that year, I joined the Usui Reiki Ryoho Gakkai upon the introduction of Ms. Onoda. In Kyoto, Koyama Sensei initiated me with the first reiju (original form of attunement) of the Dento Reiki method. Long-forgotten sensations brought me back to my spiritual home and I was moved to tears. Though I was just a newly accepted member, Koyama Sensei, 86 years old at that time, kindly offered the seat next to her to answer my questions.

As I wrote more about the Gakkai for this book, I discovered the big differences between the practices of the Dento Reiki method (based on the teachings of the Usui Reiki Ryoho Gakkai) and the practices of the Western Reiki methods, while deepening my own Reiki practices. Both were offshoots from the same root, but why were they so different? My question was whether Western Reiki had been developing or de-evolving, or even more to the point, had been converting the practice of Reiki into an entirely new thing.

In order to make it clearer to me, I learned some of the various systems and styles of the Western Reiki schools, including one from one of Hayashi Sensei's lineages, whose teachers insisted they were teaching 'Dento Reiki.' My comparative research resulted in the following findings:

1. Western Reiki methods have been changing in various ways while traveling through many countries under the influence of ethnicity and culture.
2. Dento Reiki as it was practiced by members of the Usui Reiki Ryoho Gakkai before Usui Sensei's death drastically changed after his passing and even more after the end of World War II.
3. No matter how it has been changed, we can summarize Usui Reiki by listing the two useful 技法 (Gi-ho) techniques: one that focuses on health and the other that focuses on spiritual development.
4. The heart and essence of Reiki Ryoho is 五戒 (Go-kai), which indicates the pathway to health and happiness.
5. Western Reiki is effective for pathways to health while Dento Reiki includes the key to spiritual advancement.

From about this same time period, information on Usui Sensei's life and Usui Reiki Ryoho's history, philosophy, teachings and instructions smoothly came to me one by one. It helped to clarify my understanding of what message Usui Sensei truly wanted to communicate. I sorted them out and started building a practical Reiki system only for my personal use. Naming it 現代霊気法 (Gendai Reiki Ho), which I intended to mean 'a practical Reiki method for modern people,' I kept developing it based on my experiences. In 1995, 現代霊気ヒーリング協会 (the Gendai Reiki Healing Association) was established for the purpose of properly teaching the origin and use of Reiki Ryoho that my research and experience had recognized.

I introduced the truth of Usui Sensei and his Reiki Ryoho and my personal Reiki practice in *Iyashi no Gendai Reiki Ho* in May 1998 in Japan, resulting in worldwide knowledge of Gendai Reiki Ho.

An international gathering of Reiki masters, the "Japanese Reiki Workshop," was held in Vancouver, Canada for three days in August 1999. It was organized by Reiki Masters from Japan, America, England and Canada, in cooperation with the Canadian Reiki Association. Along with about 70 Reiki Masters from seven countries, two Reiki Masters from Japan attended with me, and I spoke as a lecturer. This international sharing of so much information and so many materials about Reiki, including the facts of Usui Sensei's life and Reiki's starting point, as well as the current existence of the Usui Reiki Ryoho Gakkai, finally allowed this, the true story of Reiki to come out to the world. *Iyashi no Gendai Reiki Ho (Modern Reiki Method for Healing)* was translated into English on this occasion, and it contributed a lot to spread the above stated facts about Reiki Ryoho.

During this same time, Usui Reiki Ryoho International (URRI) was founded as an international network of Reiki Masters that, for many years, organized yearly workshops in many cities around the world including Kyoto (Japan) in 2000, Madrid (Spain) in 2001, Toronto (Canada) in 2002 and Silkeborg (Denmark) in 2003. These workshops further contributed to the dissemination of information about Reiki.

Although the URRI completed its role in Denmark in 2003, Gendai Reiki Ho continued to hold Master Special Course seminars for the attendants of the URRI workshops starting with the 2000 Kyoto workshop. The Masters who took this course were authorized as Gendai Reiki Masters, and many of them have opened Gendai Reiki schools in their countries.

Also dating from that time have come invitations to speak to a variety of Gendai Reiki groups in Canada, Spain, France, Australia, Italy, Russia and Denmark about the truth of Usui Reiki Ryoho. The number of Gendai Reiki Masters who have studied with me is now about 900 in Japan and more than 600 in 34 foreign countries.

The spread of Reiki has been accelerated in Japan. The number of practitioners is estimated to be approximately 200,000 as of January 2013. This rapid diffusion has produced an upsurge of Reiki schools with numerous claims, some of which seeming to have moved away from the true teachings and practice of Reiki. To help establish more universal and trustworthy guidelines for the practice of Reiki in Japan, a nonprofit organization called the Gendai Reiki Network (GRN) was approved by the Japanese government in April 2005. It was mainly led by Gendai Reiki Masters in order to support all Reiki Masters' progress and to contribute to society through the healthy promotion of Reiki.

GRN began its activities with Kensan-kai (study meetings) of Master members and through Koryu-kai (gatherings, Reiki shares) in some of the main cities of Japan. Through networking with Reiki Masters abroad who shared the same spirit of intention came groups such as Gendai Reiki Australia and

Gendai Reiki Italia, which quite naturally developed into the Gendai Reiki International Network. Now international exchanges with North and South American countries, the U.K., Spain, France, The Netherlands, Denmark, New Zealand and so on have been upheld in favorable ways.

A five-day international gathering of Gendai Reiki practitioners was held on March 15, 2012 in Kyoto. Originally this gathering had been planned for April 2011, but had to be postponed because of the devastating disaster that had struck Japan just before the conference's scheduled start date. However, the postponement did not change the conference's success one year later. Gendai Reiki attendees from all over the world joined together to learn about and share not only Gendai Reiki but also to collaborate with practitioners of Zen, Aikido and Nagauta (traditional stage performance), giving all of us a true feeling of strong ties with all living things.

Another wonderful result of the 2012 international gathering was the unanimous adoption of a document entitled "How Reiki is Understood in Gendai Reiki Ho." The italicized sentences below comprise what we refer to as the 'Gendai Reiki Charter.'

Reiki is the Love of the Universe.
It gives all living things the gift of life and and causes then to evolve.

Reiki is the origin of Life.
Each life is a drop of water in the ocean of life that forms a circle.

Reiki fills the Universe.
Resonance with Reiki leads us to Love, Harmony and Healing.

Utilizing Reiki is creating life.
It gives us peaceful, abundant, healthy and joyful life.

Reiki lights up our life.
The Universe always watches over us and guides us to fulfillment.

Reiki's simplicity and effectiveness as an energy healing have allowed Reiki to reach the four corners of the world. But hand-on healing is just its entrance. The ultimate goal is spiritual advancement. As we practice Reiki, it is crucial to understand Usui Sensei's teaching: that the purpose of life is to achieve a peaceful mind state and then while holding that peace within, fulfill our destined missions. According to the facts confirmed at this point in time, this book presents Usui Sensei's life, the truth of Usui Reiki Ryoho and the understandings and Gi-ho (techniques) of Gendai Reiki Ho.

I do hope that the English-speaking practitioners who read this book will relate the truth about Usui Sensei and Reiki to as many people as possible at every opportunity.

May Reiki's 波動 (hado) of Love, Harmony and Healing reach all of you.

Hiroshi Doi
January 2013

Introduction

Reiki-ho is the Technique for Healing and Enlightenment by 気[2] Ki and the Light—the Universal Energy.

Reiki-ho is a traditional way of using Ki for hands-on healing of the body and mind. 霊気, written "REIKI" in English, is a kind of superior healing technique that is found all over the world, and, although currently based mainly in America, is still spreading.

People in general have the impression that Reiki-ho is a "perfect" technique that has so many advantages such as:

1. No hard training is necessary. Soon after you receive Reiki energy, you can start "hand healing."
2. Once you get the ability, you never lose it; it remains forever.
3. Concentration is not needed. Just putting your hands on allows the energy to flow as needed.
4. The effect does not differ from the believer to the non-believer.
5. You do not take in any negative energy.

More and more people are starting to learn Reiki-ho since they acknowledge that it is an advanced technique not only for healing the mind and body but also for raising spirituality. Now Reiki-ho is also becoming popular as the healing method that does not require any difficult training or effort.

Reiki-ho is a Saving Message from the Ancients

Use of the Universal Reiki hado[3] was developed as one of the secret methods of the "shaman" in ancient times (before written history) and was used for healing and spiritual guidance, fostering interaction with the Great Nature. It had been handed down without being revealed to the public eye until being systematized and perfected by Usui Mikao in 1922 as "Usui Reiki Ryoho": the healing technique by the radiation of Light and Ki.

Since then Reiki-ho has healed many seriously sick people, and has also given "the ability to heal" to those who have wanted it. Yet, although it was founded by a Japanese, almost all Japanese people totally forgot about Reiki after WWII in Japan. Few people knew Reiki-ho before its return from

[2] 気 Ki: qi, chi, life energy, vital energy.

[3] 波動 Hado: wave, vibration, energy.

America. Now, since an American Reiki book has been published in Japanese and Reiki seminars have become available here, it has spread very quickly, along with the "Qigong boom."

The Significance of Reiki-ho's Return to Japan

Recently the number of people who are interested in Reiki-ho has increased, and that interest is spreading rapidly, since many publishers have begun to publish books about Reiki, and the spiritual magazines feature stories about Reiki-ho.

Consequently, Western Reiki schools have provided all the Reiki curricula, from the beginner's course to the teacher's course, which were not available before. Now we have much better circumstances to learn Reiki-ho here in Japan. I understand it is not merely because the time is ripe but also because Japan *needs* Reiki-ho right at this moment.

To create a peaceful and rich society, we should not be misguided by the idea of "the end-of-the-century prophecy" or seek for temporary and selfish desires. I believe that we should constantly make the effort to improve ourselves and take responsibility for our own lives.

The environment surrounding us is filled with stress and excess tension, harming the mind and body. There is no room for people to have compassion for others when those people themselves are in pain. We first must release our own unnecessary tension and learn to live in a relaxed way all the time. Reiki-ho is wonderfully effective as a relaxation method to remove stress.

Let's Understand More about Reiki-ho

Today, there are many groups and individuals who offer seminars on Reiki-ho. And the number of Reiki Masters (teachers) who can perform the "energy transmission" is gradually increasing.

When I spoke on the theme of "Teaching Traditional Reiki" on December 23, 1997 in Tokyo, it was reported that there were about 2,000 Reiki websites online.

Now, I wonder if all those Reiki Masters have the same ability. Do they provide seminars of the same quality? Why are there differences in the duration of seminars and curricula? Are Dento Reiki, founded by Usui Sensei, and Western Reiki the same? How are the attunements performed? And there are many other questions we might ask, yet no clear answer is given to those who want to learn now.

I also wonder if there are enough follow-up classes provided to the seminar-takers so that they can keep improving after the seminar. What if someone says, "It seems like it works, but actually, I am not quite sure" or "I was taught that I did not get negative energy, but I feel pain each time I give Reiki healing"? How do you guide and teach *them*?

Through my experiences, I will try to answer these questions in this book, hoping that all my readers will understand.

Self-purifying and Self-growth Giho[4]

The five characteristics of Reiki-ho I mentioned are only part of the story. The real quality of Reiki-ho is not that easy to set out in words.

If you do not understand the depth of Reiki-ho, you might get the wrong idea—that it is just a teaching that does not require any effort to learn more about beyond the initial class or a technique that merely develops and satisfies some egotistic purpose that makes you arrogant and proud. This kind of attitude is far from the truth about the use of Reiki-ho, and there should be no need to even state this because the *essence* of Reiki-ho cannot be defined only as the development of healing ability. It must be used for self-purifying and self-growth to complete "the necessary lesson" all day and every day.

Part I. "This is Reiki-ho" provides a digest of the basic knowledge, which is useful for people who have already learned Reiki and also for those who want to start now.

Part II. "Q & A about Reiki-ho" consists of questions and answers for deeper comprehension of Reiki-ho.

Part III. "Self-Purifying and Self-Growth Giho" introduces the Giho and its procedures for self-purifying and self-growth, and also offers various kinds of useful Giho for self-development. 発霊法 Hatsurei-ho, the Giho that Usui Sensei taught, is especially useful as an exercise to enhance your ability and raise your spirituality.

I am happy and willing to introduce more utilization of Reiki when you finish those steps and want to learn more. This ultimate utilization will help you get closer to *Satori*, the enlightenment that Usui Sensei reached.

However, it would also be my great pleasure if this book could encourage one more person to understand and practice the truth of Reiki-ho.

土居 裕 Hiroshi Doi
February 1998

4 技法 Giho: method, technique, exercise, training.

癒しの
現代霊気法

PART I

THIS IS REIKI-HO
THE REIKI DIGEST

Chapter I

Reiki and Reiki-ho

Hand Healing: A Natural Healing Method Begun in Ancient Times

Since prehistoric times in the East and the West, people have been aware of the mysterious energy that radiates from "the human palm." When we have a stomachache or headache, are bruised or injured, we put hands on the affected areas almost as a reflex. This action is instinctive. People have known through experience that this action sometimes removes or reduces pain.

Furthermore, it was found that the effectiveness often depended on *whose* hands. Particular people possessed much more healing power than others. This instinctive reaction came to be systematized as "hand healing" in order to develop healing skill. The skilled healers touched or held hands over the patient's body to sense the imbalanced areas and quickly relieve the pains and symptoms. In this way "hand healing" became an effective natural treatment and important remedy in primitive medicine.

It is recorded in a variety of literature that the Buddha and Christ healed sick people by laying on hands and that it was performed in ancient Greece and Rome. It is also said that the European kings healed sick people by "Royal Touch," which simply meant to touch the patients.

What is Reiki-ho?

The Reiki-ho I introduce in this book starts with the healing method that uses the power from the hands, the same way as other hand healings that have existed from ancient times. It differs, however, from other similar healing methods in the respect that a difficult training period is not necessary and anyone can perform the healing easily just by following the system. Furthermore, its distinctive aspect is that this practice of healing allows anyone to live life fully by harnessing the energy of the Universe.

Reiki-ho was originally established as "Usui Reiki Ryoho" by Usui Mikao (1865–1926) in 1922 (the 11th year of Taisho[5]) as "the way to make mind and body healthy on the basis of the Universal Reiki." Usui Reiki Ryoho

[5] 大正 Taisho period: 1912 –1926.

became wide spread in Japan as a very effective hand healing method, and it was adopted by many people, especially those in the Japanese Navy due to the support of Rear Admirals Ushida and Taketomi.

Reiki Ryoho was brought over to the United States in 1938 after Usui Sensei's death, and became popular during the time of the developing New Age Movement. Reiki in the United States developed independently from the original Japanese style, becoming known as "REIKI, the healing technique for mind and body." It was disseminated abroad from its base in America and landed back in Japan in the late 1980s as "Reiki-ho."

Reiki Ryoho was born in Japan, traveled through many countries and rapidly progressed, with diverse transformations. Now it has grown up to be a superior healing technique, and also an effective way for gaining the spiritual advancement that leads to a full life. Numerous styles have been developed.

Reiki is the Universal Energy

Usui Sensei said, *"Everything that exists in the Universe possesses Reiki."* Reiki is the Universal energy, the source of all existence, the hado of Love and the pure Light that comes from a higher dimension.

The Great Universe (Mother Nature) revolves and circulates with no stagnation. We humans are a "microcosm" that share the same origin with Mother Nature and live by resonating with the hado of the "macrocosm." What connects "microcosm" and "macrocosm" is the hado of Love called "the Universal energy."

The Universal energy exists in everything; it is the life energy inside the human body that gives us natural healing ability and the power to live with vigor. The life energy is known by a variety of names such as aura, Ki, vitality, Reiki, Reishi, life magnetism, prana, body radioactivity and so on. As we are "the lord of creation," humans possess more Reiki than any other creature and radiate auras vigorously.

Active Use of the Universal Energy

Reiki-ho is a technique that enables one to heal everything he or she sees and/or touches by connecting to Reiki—the Universal energy as well as the hado of Love—and becoming a channel for it. To become a channel for Reiki, you have to receive the hado of Love by uniting yourself with the consciousness and the rhythm of the Universe and by purifying yourself to transmit it as it is.

Learning Reiki-ho starts when you are given Reiki energy from an instructor (Master/teacher/ 師範 Shihan,[6] etc.) by means of an "energy transmission," which enables you to connect with Reiki anytime and anywhere you need it to perform healing.

The energy transmission is given to each person in a respectful manner, following the standardized method called a Reiki attunement. It opens a pathway of Reiki energy inside you that aligns your resonance, the microcosm, with the vibration of the macrocosm. In this way, you become able to connect with the Universal energy (Reiki) anytime you want to use it.

The Hado of Love from a Higher Dimension

Now, the phrase "Universal energy" is used with various meanings. Some people claim that they have found unknown energy and call it "XX energy" or "XX power." The usage of it depends on the person: for his future, self-fulfillment, satisfaction and so on. But the substance of these energies is not entirely clarified: some of them are the same as Reiki and some are not. The only difference between Reiki and non-Reiki energy is whether it is the "hado of Love," whether it leads everything to Life and Harmony or does not.

I define Reiki, the Universal energy, as the power that gave birth to the Great Universe, created the solar system, brought about all the creatures on the earth and maintains them in good order. It is also the foundation of the source energy of all manifestation in the Universe. This is the fine energy vibration (hado of Love) radiating to the Universe from the highest consciousness with the purpose to carry out its will.

What is the Hado of Love?

What then is the hado of Love? The interpretation of "love" might depend on the person interpreting it. My definition is "the life energy emanating from the higher consciousness and spreading outwards equally in all directions."

Love is, for example, like the sun. You might argue, "The sun is substance; it does not possess consciousness." But quantum physics has elucidated for us that everything has its own consciousness. The sun constantly emits the life energy in every direction to all creatures. This energy is heat, light and hado. This is one example of how the hado of Love emanates from the Universe.

We usually perceive the "material" sun, but actually, the "spiritual" sun constantly radiates the healing energy to us.

[6] 師範 Shihan: teacher, master, instructor.

The hado of affection is similar to the hado of Love. But since it contains a person's emotions, its energy is directed towards a certain object. When the person sublimates the energy to radiate equally in all directions, it turns out to be the hado of Love.

The Universal Energy is Everywhere as Hado

How are we involved with the Universal energy? There are countless stars twinkling in the sky as far as the eye can see. These stars, the solar system, are just a part of the vast universe. It is considered that about 100 billion of those that are as big as the solar system exist in the galactic system and about 100 billion of those as big as the galactic system exist in the universe. The "Big Bang," the beginning of the universe, was worked on by the Universal energy.

The Universal energy created the sun, the moon, the earth and its oceans, bred its creatures and evolved mankind. The Universal energy exists as the life energy in an entire plant as well as in a single grain. Humanity, one part of the Universe, is sustained by this life energy. The Universal energy fills the Universe in the form of hado. Modern science confirms that all the beings are hado and that every existence has a different frequency of vibration yet shares the same nature.

We are in good state of mind and body when we are on the same wavelength as the Great Universe. It enables us to "follow our excitement" - Bashar. When our body and mind are on different wavelengths from the Universe, we lose our health of body and mind, and suffer with misfortune.

From this perspective, Reiki does not "change our nature" but lets us tune to the hado of the Universe and supports us to "return to what we should be." It also eliminates disharmony in the body and mind at every level and helps us complete our "necessary spiritual lessons."

Now, it is time to learn how to use it.

Characteristics of Reiki-ho

Let me introduce the characteristics of Reiki-ho. I think many persons and groups who are spreading Reiki-ho have already described its qualities as attractive characteristics. Here, I bring them together into eleven points with explanations, which I think is necessary to prevent any misunderstandings brought about by superficial interpretation.

(1) No training is necessary—Anybody can perform healing from the moment the pathway of Reiki is opened by the attunement.

The healing ability is given without any training. You, however, must continue to purify yourself and heighten your spirituality to develop the healing ability and to become an ever clearer pathway of Reiki energy.

(2) The ability is never lost—You will never lose the ability once the pathway of Reiki is opened even if it is not used at all.

The ability you obtain from the attunement is basic and only the first step; whether you can develop it or not depends on your self-discipline. In other words, your ability is not lost, but stays at the beginner's level if you do not use it at all.

(3) The power increases—The more you use the Reiki healing ability, the stronger and more powerful it becomes. You never get tired by healing.

The more you use it, the stronger it gets, and at the same time, your mind and body and that of its other recipients also get healed. But it is fundamental that you must recognize yourself as a channel of Reiki. If you have an illusion that you "have" this great power or try to strengthen the healing effect with your consciousness, you can lose your life energy and health.

(4) No concentration or effort is necessary—Reiki automatically flows as much as needed when your hands are put on (held over) the body.

Concentration or condensation of 念 Nen[7] must not be done. It is crucial to relax and place the hands without any intentions.

(5) No bad energy gets carried—As Reiki is a clear Light, it neither sends out nor brings in bad energy.

As long as the pathway of Reiki energy is clean, there is no need to worry about it. Place your 心 *Kokoro*[8] in 丹田 the Tanden,[9] the lower abdomen, and maintain your consciousness at a high level to prevent tuning into negative hado.

(6) It is effective regardless of one's belief—No matter what religion or ideology you follow, or whether or not you believe in Reiki, it brings about the effects.

---

7 念 Nen: Strong will, strong desire, emotional force, intention, intense concentration, strong control by mind or consciousness. As Nen tend to be used to satisfy ego or selfish desire, Reiki healers are taught not to use it while healing.

8 心 Kokoro: self, whole, feeling, emotion, spirit, soul, mind, heart, faith, consciousness, personality, idea, philosophy.

9 丹田 Tanden: the lower abdomen, 3 – 5 centimeters below the navel.

As Reiki is effective on unconscious people, pets or plants, it does not matter whether you believe it or not. People, however, have the right to reject it. You should not impose Reiki on anyone, as the energy would not flow to the person who rejects it.

(7) It is effective on any creature—Reiki healing is effective on all creatures: humans, animals and plants, and it can be used to cleanse the energy of places as well as substances such as minerals.

Reiki works on all the creatures and beings in the Universe. However, it is important to keep your consciousness clear at all times so that you do not carelessly tune to negative or rough hado.

(8) It is synergistically effective with other methods—When you use Reiki with medical or other techniques (acupuncture, moxibustion, Qigong, chiropractic, energy work, etc.), it can produce synergistic effects.

Reiki revitalizes the life energy and enhances the natural healing ability. It facilitates any sort of medical or other techniques to manifest its true capabilities. But Reiki cannot be used with any technique that requires your conscious intention to control something.

(9) Reiki transcends space and time—Reiki enables you to perform healing from a distance, towards the present, past or future, by using the symbols.

All existence is hado. You and others are One, the same being, and there is no divider in time and space in reality. The Reiki symbols are useful until you reach a certain level, but they will become unnecessary once you understand the essence of Reiki-ho.

(10) It purifies karma—Reiki is useful for purifying karma and healing trauma. It effectively improves DNA.

Negative karma from the past, which is affecting the present life, must be cleared off to actualize true happiness. To do so, you must repeatedly self-purify with Reiki energy to extinguish those karmas and at the same time, you must live your present life without creating any new karma.

(11) It is a milestone toward spiritual awakening—You can achieve self-realization by tuning in to the source of Reiki through self-purifying and meditating, and resonate with Reiki on a daily basis.

The essence of Reiki-ho is to reach the stage of spiritual awakening—Satori, which Usui Sensei accomplished—by following the guidance of Reiki in your daily life. In other words, it is self-fulfillment in quiet, peaceful and supreme bliss.

Chapter 2

The Structure of Gendai Reiki Ho

Four Steps of Reiki-ho

Usui Reiki Ryoho Gakkai has three levels to learn: 初伝 *Sho-den*, 奥伝 *Oku-den* and 神秘伝 *Shinpi-den*. By adding the fourth level (teacher training course) to it, most of the recent Reiki-ho systems/schools employ a four-step curriculum, which students can learn one at a time to deepen their understandings more smoothly. (Gendai Reiki Ho adopts this standard four-step system, while some schools have five or more.)

Let me briefly introduce what you learn in each step of Gendai Reiki Ho.

Level I – Acquiring Healing Ability

To open the Reiki pathway, energy transmissions (commonly called attunements) are performed three times. While this English word means "to tune up the wavelength," the attunement in Reiki-ho means "to set up the conditions to connect with Reiki energy and become a pathway for it by following a particular procedure." It opens the channel that enables you to connect to Reiki whenever you need it.

From this point on, you can start the flow of the necessary energy automatically by putting your hands on (or holding the hands over). In the seminar, you learn the basic theories and healing techniques. You can use Reiki that very same day.

Although it depends on each school and teacher, you basically learn and practice in Level I as follows (I introduce here the curriculum of the Gendai Reiki Healing Association.):

1) Summary of Reiki-ho (origins, history, philosophy, structure, the attunement, etc.)
2) Basis of healing (how to use hands, aura cleansing, the basic 12 hand positions, etc.)
3) Reiki healing for people (self-healing and healing for others)
4) An understanding of the Reiki session
5) Reiki healing of animals and plants
6) Purifying and infusing energy (how to cleanse a place, room, lucky charm, stone, jewelry; how to charge energy; how to cut off negative energy)

7) Typical healing techniques (Reiki Marathon, Reiki Circle, *Nentatsu-ho*, etc.)
8) Self-purifying and Self-growth *Giho*; *Kenyoku-ho* (dry bathing), *Chakra Kassei Kokyu*[10]*-ho* (Chakra Activation Breathing), *Hikari no Kokyu-ho* (Light Breathing), *Gassho Kokyu-ho* (Gassho Breathing), etc.
9) How to practice Reiki-ho after finishing the Level I seminar.

Level II – More Powerful and Diverse Healing Results

One symbol and its accompanying *Kotodama* are given in one attunement. You take it three times in Level II, which, consequently, initiates you to three symbols and three Kotodamas in all. Please understand the Reiki symbol as a "shape or letter," and Kotodama as a "voice or sound." Both symbol and Kotodama allow you to harness Reiki energy with more potentiality.

First, the attunements in Level II enhance the quality of Reiki energy within you. Some Western Reiki schools say that the healing power becomes almost twice as strong.

Secondly, by using the symbols and Kotodamas, you can use Reiki in an infinite number of ways: for example, you can send powerful energy onto a particular point, send balanced and harmonious energy into your feelings and emotions and perform healing beyond time and space, connecting your consciousness to a distant place, in the past or future in addition to the present.

In Level II you learn and practice in as follows:

1) The basis of healing with the Reiki symbol and Kotodama
2) The first symbol (Power) and its usage
3) The second symbol (Harmony) and its usage
4) The third symbol (Absentee) and its usage
    (1) Distant healing
    (2) Healing for the past (Healing trauma from the past; cleansing karma)
    (3) Healing for the future (Sending Reiki energy for yourself in the future; setting up a desirable self-image or situations)
5) Some major techniques from abroad (Reiki box, Deprogramming, Grounding)
6) Traditional Japanese Giho

[10] 呼吸 Kokyu: breathing.

7) Self-purifying and Self-growth Giho; *Hatsurei-ho, Jiko Joka* Healing (Self-Purifying Healing,) *Saibo Kassei-ka Giho* (Cell Activation Technique)
8) How to practice Reiki-ho after finishing a Level II seminar

Level III – Live Creatively with Heightened Awareness

The fourth symbol and its Kotodama are given by three attunements. This greatly changes the quality of the energy flow inside you; it becomes as fine and subtle as the higher dimensional energy. Many people begin feeling a calmness and peace of mind. Some feel a kind of nostalgic sweetness. The energy works on the body and the consciousness to connect and unite them with the Light of the higher dimension.

The fourth symbol, called the Usui Symbol or Master Symbol, is the supreme symbol of Reiki-ho and considered very sacred overseas. When you reach this level, you will consider Reiki as the hado that guides you to spiritual awareness, and you will want to resonate with Reiki all the time to help you advance yourself through your daily life. Reiki is not just a technique for you anymore. Instead, you reach the highest level of energy, and your self-cleansing and healing ability make remarkable progress.

You learn and practice in Level III as follows:

1) The meaning and usage of the fourth symbol (Master Symbol)
2) How to connect to the higher dimension (The consciousness of the higher dimension, Higher-Self, etc.)
3) How to deepen your meditation and raise yourself (Meditation, Affirmation, etc.)
4) Usui Sensei's essence of Reiki-ho (His philosophy and teachings)
5) Achieving the milestones to spiritual awakenings (Making use of Reiki in daily life; hints for a creative life)
6) Instruction in Dento Reiki's Giho
7) Self-purifying and Self-growth Giho; *Hado Kokyu-ho* (Hado Breathing), *Hado Meiso-ho* (Hado Meditation), etc.

Level IV – Mastership Training

This is a training course for Reiki Masters who wish to become teachers. You learn how to perform the attunement and to instruct in the usage of Reiki-ho for the people who want to learn it.

It is rather easy to teach the techniques only. However, you must continue to devote yourself to the study after the completion of this course, as it is impossible to give clear energy just by knowing how to perform the attunements. Some of those conscientious and honest schools supply support for the teachers through *Koryu-kai* (gathering) and/or *Kensan-kai.*[11]

You learn and practice in Level IV as follows:

1) The theory and practice of the attunement
2) How to behave and live life as a Reiki Master (teacher)
3) The understanding and usage of the symbols and the Kotodamas
4) What to teach in each level
5) Preparation for a Reiki seminar
6) The Giho of Dento Reiki
7) *Reiju* (Japanese attunement)
8) The integrated attunement with all four symbols for a new Reiki Master

What to Learn and Obtain in Each Step

Let me summarize each step from the point of view of what you can learn and obtain. First of all, you have to understand that Reiki-ho is "simple."

The first step is the beginners' course; it contains a lot of information and practice to help students understand Reiki correctly. But as you go up to the higher levels, the way becomes generally less detailed and simpler. You do not need to acquire all the skills you are taught. The basic Giho you must learn are very few. After going through all the Giho, just choose and apply some of them when they are suitable to your personal needs.

In Level I, you open the pathway of Reiki through three attunements, and you learn techniques such as healing the mind and body as well as purifying the energy. In other words, you get the Reiki healing ability and learn how to use it.

Next, in Level II, three attunements focus the power and quality of Reiki within you. These attunements enable you to use the Reiki symbols and the Kotodamas to perform higher level techniques such as healing beyond time and space, power concentration and regaining mental balance. In short, you raise your healing ability and expand the usage of Reiki with symbolized healing.

[11] 研鑽会 Kensan-kai: study meeting to share techniques and information, and to teach and learn from each other.

In Level III, you connect yourself with the Light of the higher dimension and reach the highest level of hado through three attunements. You can also connect to the consciousness of the Universe with the Master Symbol, and develop yourself through the presence of its guidance in your daily life. In other words, Level III is the supreme usage of Reiki; we move through to the self-realization of being constantly supported and guided by the Love of the Universe on an everyday basis.

The Attunement

Let me give you a simple explanation of the attunement.

When Usui Sensei mastered how to heal with Reiki along with his spiritual awakening after his 21 days of fast on Mt. Kurama in Kyoto, he thought, "This power should not be monopolized in a single family. I must spread it to people at large." As a result of his research of numerous pieces of literature and study, he completed reiju, the technique of energy transmission, and Hatsurei-ho, the exercise to accelerate Reiki flow.

He established the Usui Reiki Ryoho Gakkai and performed the Sho-den energy transmission, giving the healing ability to anyone who wanted it. The very first reiju was performed in Harajuku in Tokyo, then it went over to the United States and there, transformed into the attunement.

The English word "attunement" means, according to the dictionary, "to tune into the same wavelengths of radio." It also means "to tune the musical instruments" or "to share the mental wavelength, emotions and feelings." I guess they started adopting this word to express "to tune with the Universe." Some Reiki Masters (teachers) call it "initiation" instead. In modern parlance, one could say "to open the chakras." (They do not mean exactly the same thing though.)

When performing the attunement, Reiki Masters first clear the receiver, connect with Reiki and surround themselves with the Light. Then the Masters set up the flowing line of Reiki from the receiver's crown to the sacrum along the receiver's spine. They send Reiki into the particular points of the flowing line and accelerate the flow. They then send the excess Reiki off from the feet into the ground, and perform a tuning so that the receiver's palms radiate strong healing energy and can adjust the energy automatically.

In Level II and the higher levels, Reiki Masters set up the receiver's conditions of each point to resonate with the hado of the Universe when the receivers use the symbols and the Kotodamas.

All of the above should be performed thoroughly by Masters who are capable of sending clear and fine Reiki energy, and this is considered "the essence of Reiki-ho."

Chapter 3

Reiki History

Mikao Usui: the Founder of Usui Reiki Ryoho

The personal history of the founder, Usui Sensei, is passed on semi-legendarily; the facts are not confirmed much in detail. Especially when Reiki-ho went overseas, many stories were made up while spreading from its base in the United States. The trustworthy record is 臼井先生功徳之碑[12,13] (Usui Sensei Koutoku No Hi), the epitaph of Usui Sensei's merit and virtue, found at 西方寺 (Saiho-ji Temple) in Tokyo. This monument was erected on February 2, 1927, one year after his death, by some of his over 2,000 students. The following is an English translation of its interpretation into modern Japanese by me:

Usui Sensei Koutoku No Hi

"What you naturally learn through self-discipline and training is 徳 (virtue), and it is 功 (merit) to voluntarily practice to lead and save people. The person who has many merits and a good deal of virtue can be eventually respected as a great founder. From old times, those who started up new studies and religions—sages, philosophers or geniuses—were like as mentioned above. We can say that Usui Sensei is one of those magnificent leaders.

He started a new method to improve the body and mind based on the Reiki of the Universe. His reputation attracted people from all around the country at once who wanted to learn Reiki and recieve treatments. Really, it was very successful indeed.

Usui Sensei—first name 甕男Mikao and pen name 暁帆 Gyohan—was from 谷合村 Taniai-village, 山形郡 Yamagata-county, 岐阜県 Gifu-prefecture. His forefather was Tsunetane Chiba, who had played an active part as a military commander between the end of Heian Period and the beginning

[12] 功徳 Koutoku: merit and virtuous deed.

[13] 碑 Hi: monument, memorial stone, tombstone, gravestone.

of Kamakura Period. His father's name was 胤氏 Taneuji, but was commonly called 宇左衛門 Uzaemon. His mother was from the Kawai family. Usui Sensei was born on August 15, the first year of Keio.[14] Having studied while working since childhood, he made great efforts to be far superior to his friends.

After growing up, he went over to Europe and America, and studied in China. In spite of his ability, however, he was not always successful in his career advancement. Although he often led a poor life, he strove much more than before to polish his body and mind without flinching from the difficulties.

One day, Usui Sensei climbed 鞍馬山 Mt. Kurama, where he began to do an ascetic practice while fasting. Suddenly on the twenty-first day, he felt a great Reiki over his head. He was given Satori and Reiki Ryoho at the same time. When he tried it on his own body and with his family, it brought immediate effects. He said, "I must share this power with the general public and enjoy the benefits with them rather than keep it exclusively inside my family." Usui Sensei moved to Aoyama Harajuku, Tokyo in April, the eleventh year of Taisho (1922), and established the Gakkai, where Reiki Ryoho was instructed openly to the public and the treatment was given too. People visited him from far and near to ask for his guidance and cure and they overflowed outside of the Gakkai building making a long line.

In September of the twelfth year of Taisho (1923), Tokyo had a very big fire caused by the Great Kanto Earthquake, when the injured and sick suffered from pains everywhere. Usui Sensei felt deep sympathy for them and gave treatments, going around the city every day. We can hardly calculate how many people were saved from death through his devotion. This is just a brief description of his relief activity, in which he extended his hands of love over suffering people in an emergency.

As his training center became too small to receive the visitors, he built a new treatment house and moved to Nakano, outside the city, in February the fourteenth year of Taisho (1925). Gaining a growing reputation, he was often invited from everywhere throughout Japan. In accordance with these requests, he traveled to Kure and Hiroshima, then entered Saga and reached Fukuyama. When he was staying at an inn there, he unexpectedly became sick and passed away there at the age of sixty-two.[15]

[14] 慶応 Keio period: 1865 –1868; the first year of Keio was 1865.

[15] According to the old Japanese way of counting age he was 62. In the present counting, he was 60 in March 1926.

His wife, Sadako, from the Suzuki family, had a son and a daughter with him. Their son's name was 不二 Fuji, and he succeeded the Usui family.

Usui Sensei's natural character was gentle and modest, and he never showed off. His body was big and sturdy, and his face was always filled with a warm smile. But when he confronted difficulties, he went ahead with a strong will and persevered well, yet kept extremely careful. He was a man of versatile talents, and also a book lover, possessing a great deal of information on a wide range of subjects, from history, biography, medical science, and from the canons of Christianity, Buddhism and psychology to the magic of the ascetic, the art of the curse, the science of divination and physiognomy. It was evident to everybody that Usui Sensei's cultivation and self-discipline were based on his career of art and science, and this cultivation and self-discipline became a clue to the tenets of Reiki Ryoho.

Reiki Ryoho is aiming not only at how to heal diseases but also at how to correct *Kokoro*, keep the body healthy, and to enjoy the happiness of life by a God-sent spiritual ability. Therefore, when teaching, we first let the students understand the last instructions of the Meiji[16] Emperor[17], and chant 五戒 *Go-kai* morning and evening to keep them in mind.

The Go-kai says: Today, 1) do not be angry, 2) do not worry, 3) be thankful, 4) do what you are meant to do, 5) be kind to others. These are truly important precepts for mental cultivation, just the same as those by which the ancient sages admonished themselves. Usui Sensei attributed Go-kai as being the secret to inviting in happiness and the miraculous medicine that cures all diseases. He clearly showed his purpose of teaching the Go-kai. Furthermore, he tried to teach as easily and simply as possible—so nothing was difficult to understand. Each time you sit quietly and *Gassho* and chant Go-kai morning and evening, you aid in the development of a pure and sound mind, and this is the essence for making the most of this in your daily life. This is the reason why Reiki Ryoho is accepted very easily by everybody.

The social situation is very changeable these days, and people's thoughts are apt to change, too. If we would most fortunately succeed in spreading Reiki Ryoho everywhere, we feel sure that it would certainly be very helpful in preventing people from disordering their moral sense. Its benefits stretch even farther than the curing of long term illnesses, chronic diseases and bad habits.

---

[16] 明治 Meiji period: 1868 –1912.

[17] 明治天皇 Meiji Emperor: 1852 –1912.

The number of students who learned from Usui Sensei amounts to more than 2,000 persons. Some leading students in Tokyo are taking over his work in the training center, while other pupils outside of Tokyo also do everything to popularize Reiki Ryoho. Although our teacher already passed away, we have to do the very best to hand Reiki Ryoho down to the public forever and spread it much more. Ah! What a great thing he did; he generously shared what he had experienced by himself!

As a result of our recent meeting and discussion, we decided to erect a memorial stone at the graveyard in his family temple so that we could share his virtuous deeds and leave them for posterity; I was asked to write the epitaph on the monument. As I was deeply impressed by our Sensei's great meritorious deeds and also struck by the students' warm hearts in a bond with our Sensei, I dared not refuse the request, but described the outline on it. Therefore, I do expect from the heart that people in the future will look up at this monument with boundless admiration and deep respect for our Sensei.

February, the 2nd year of Showa[18]

Edited by Masayuki Okada,
The Junior 3rd Rank, the 3rd Order of Merit, Doctor of Literature
Calligraphy by Juzaburo Ushida,
The Junior 4th Rank, the 3rd Order of Merit, the 4th Class of Services, Rear Admiral

(Translated into modern Japanese by Hiroshi Doi, Ashiya City, on 1st January, 1998)
(Translated into English by Tetsuyuki Ono, Takarazuka City, on 19th June, 1998)

Pursuit in Life and Awakening on Mt. Kurama

The memorial stone says that Usui Sensei worked his way through many studies and broadened his view by going to the Western countries and China several times. Following his instincts, he experienced a variety of occupations such as bureaucrat, office worker, entrepreneur, journalist, politician's secretary, missionary, supervisor of prisoners and so on. As he faced both sides of society through his experiences and studies, he explored the greatest theme: "What is the purpose of life?"

18 昭和 Showa period: 1926 –1989. The 2nd year of Showa was 1927.

As a result of his devotion to his studies he concluded that the ultimate purpose of life is to get 安心立命 *An-shin Ritsu-mei*. The dictionary explains: "Anshin Ritsumei is to know and accept one's 天命 *Tenmei* (fate) and maintain peaceful 心 Kokoro and be free from everything" and "天命 Tenmei (fate) is destiny you cannot control." So, Anshin Ritsumei can be explained in this way: "After you have done everything you had to do, you should leave what you cannot change to the Universe and keep peaceful Kokoro without worrying about anything at all." This understanding is what is considered as Usui Sensei's "first Satori."

Satori is to know the truth (ultimate reality) by leaving behind the ego and reaching eternal joy. There are some steps necessary to reach this state. "The first Satori" is the intellectual one gotten by the self-consciousness. At this stage, it is understood only by the mind, and it is not yet a true awakening. A true Satori is an intuitive experience by *Shinga* (spirit, Higher-Self), which completes the unity with the truth.

Usui Sensei went into Zen practice and trained himself for three years to experience the state of "Anshin Ritsumei." In spite of all those trainings, he could not attain spiritual enlightenment and asked his teacher of Zen how he should keep practicing to reach the true Satori.

The teacher responded immediately, "Well, why don't you die once?" As Usui Sensei was advised to "die" from his only moorings, he prepared for death and started fasting on Mt. Kurama. It was in February 1922. At midnight after three weeks, he felt a great shock in the center of the brain, as if being struck by lightning, and lost consciousness for some hours.

It was dawn when he became conscious, and he found that he was filled with an extreme refreshment that he had never felt before. When he had felt the great shock in his brain, Reiki of the Universe had pierced his body and mind, and he had resonated with Reiki in his body. He experienced a sense of oneness with the Universe: *"I am the Universe. The Universe is me."* He had finally completed the true awakening.

Running down from the mountain with joy, he tripped on the root of a tree and fell and broke his toenail. When he put his hand on the toe as a reflex action, the pain was quickly removed and it cured immediately. This was the beginning of his healing experience. Usui Sensei not only relieved suffering and diseases from many people, but he also developed the technique that gave this ability to large numbers of people after his continuous, dedicated study.

Usui Sensei, who was born to be a generous and open-minded person, became able to put himself into the perfect state of selflessness anytime and anywhere from the moment of this Satori on Mt. Kurama.

In April 1922, he developed the teachings and a system of instruction and established the Usui Reiki Ryoho Gakkai. He began healing people who had mental and physical diseases by using Reiki Ryoho. He also gave the healing ability by energy transmission to anyone who wanted it. He continued guiding and providing the purpose for Usui Reiki Ryoho Gakkai—not only to raise the healing ability of his students but also to maintain the health of self and others, as well as to enhance the happiness and prosperity of family, society, the nation and the world, while improving oneself.[19]

Successors in Japan

Usui Sensei continues to be admired as "the restorer of hand healing" by later generations all over the world, right up to the present day. It is said that millions of people have been saved by Reiki. During his own time, Usui Sensei was renowned all over Japan. In addition to the people that he gave Reiki to, the records show that more than 2,000 people were given the Reiki Ryoho ability from Usui Sensei. But among those who finished Sho-den and Oku-den, only 21 people were permitted to progress to Shinpi-den.[20] The distinctive aspect about those who progressed to Shinpi-den is that many of them were officers in the Japanese Navy, such as Rear Admiral Juzaburo Ushida, Rear Admiral Kan'ichi Taketomi, Rear Admiral Tetsutaro Imaizumi, Vice Admiral Wanami Hoichi and Captain Chujiro Hayashi. The Japanese Navy provided three of Usui Reiki Ryoho Gakkai's presidents from its top officers: Ushida, Taketomi and Wanami.

Chujiro Hayashi Sensei (1879–1940) had been practicing diligently as a member of the Gakkai from the time he was in the Navy. He was given Shinpi-den from Usui Sensei in 1925, the 14th year of Taisho period, after his retirement from the navy. As Usui Sensei passed away the next year, Hayashi Sensei was the last Shinpi-den practitioner certified directly by Usui Sensei. He founded 林霊気研究会 *Hayashi Reiki Kenkyu-kai* (research center) and opened his Reiki clinic in Shinano-machi, Tokyo, under Usui Sensei's instructions to develop Reiki Ryoho. The clinic had eight treatment beds and

[19] The story has been passed down within the Usui Reiki Ryoho Gakkai. It is also written in 「会員のための霊気療法のしおり」 *Kaiin no tame no Reiki Ryoho no Shiori (Guide of Reiki Ryoho for the members)*, September 1st, 1974. Editor: Shinshin Kaizen Usui Reiki Ryoho Gakkai Head Office. The representative issuer: Hoichi Wanami. Sold at cost only to Gakkai members. This is the B6-size leaflet. The story is written in the section of 「本会の歴史」 *Honkai no Reikishi (The History of Our Gakkai.)*

[20] Some sources indicate this number to be 20.

each patient was treated by two healers. It is said that the clinic was successful and always very busy, eventually employing 16 healers. Hayashi Sensei left the Gakkai after Usui Sensei passed away, but he worked actively according to Usui Sensei's wishes until WWII broke out.

From Japan to the World

There was a woman named Hawayo Takata (1900–1980) who had made a dramatic recovery from life threatening diseases by receiving Reiki Ryoho at Hayashi Sensei's clinic. She was a *Nisei* (a person born to Japanese parents in another country; considered to be second-generation), born in Hawaii. In 1935 she came back to Japan, her parents' homeland. She was a widow with two little daughters when she was diagnosed with serious diseases and told that she did not have much time left. Her doctor referred her to Hayashi Sensei's clinic. By being given Reiki there, she was restored to health in two months and completely recovered after eight months. She was deeply impressed with this and worked at Hayashi Sensei's clinic for a year as his student before she went back to Hawaii with her daughters. She received Shinpi-den when Hayashi Sensei visited Hawaii in 1938 and then started her Reiki clinic. She devoted herself mostly to giving Reiki and had seldom done energy transmissions. However, she started giving attunements about five years before her death and had trained 22 instructors before she passed away at the age of 80. These 22 instructors trained by Takata Sensei have spread Reiki all over the world and over three million people received the attunements in the first dozen years or so after this, and the number of the practitioners is still increasing.

Takata Sensei passed away in December 1980. One year later, 17 Reiki Masters taught by Takata Sensei came together in Hawaii for a week. In that year (1981), the Reiki Alliance was formed by this same group of Reiki Masters. Although most of the Reiki Masters joined this group, Barbara Ray, who had a different opinion about Reiki, established the American International Reiki Association (later the Radiance Technique). In this way, the Reiki current from Takata Sensei was split into two major streams.

In addition to its popularity in the United States, Reiki is also becoming popular in Canada, Britain, Australia, Germany, Spain, France, Brazil, Russia, India and many other countries. In India, a group of Osho (Bhagwan Shree Rajneesh) adopted Reiki from Ms. Furumoto's group. They are promoting it as "Osho Reiki." In the late 1980s, Reiki teachings of many streams were brought back to Japan and it has grown in popularity here as well. It seems to be traveling to Taiwan and Korea from Japan.

Usui Reiki Ryoho, born in Japan, was developed through Chujiro Hayashi Sensei's own style and as such, was taught to Hawayo Takata Sensei. In this way it expanded all over the world through her twenty-two Masters. However, Hawayo Takata Sensei changed the Hayashi style, simplifying it by eliminating many of the special techniques and developing a simplified hand position system. She also added the use of the Usui Master symbol. I call this current "Western Reiki." You might discover stories and legends that were made up while it went through so many countries—one in particular, how Usui Sensei was given "divine revelation" on Mt. Kurama, is described dramatically, like a scene from a movie. But I think the above explanations cover enough information to know Reiki's history.

Back to Japan as Reiki-ho

While most Japanese did not know even the name Reiki until just a few years ago, since the early 1980s, it has spread quickly through the Western countries, along with the New Age movement. In part, that is how it came back to Japan in the late 1980s as a totally new healing technique.

Ms. Mieko Mitsui, a journalist from New York, translated Dr. Barbara Ray's book, *The Reiki Factor*, into Japanese and gave it the title, *Reiki Ryoho* and introduced it to Japan. Her seminar which billed her as the first Japanese-authorized Reiki teacher, attracted many people and it became a kind of boom. I appreciate that she played a great role in re-introducing Reiki to Japan.

The "advantage-only" seminars drew in many people, even those who were half in doubt because they provided a lot of attractive merits: "only one attunement gives you healing ability," "no need of strict discipline," "no need of effort," "no need of concentration," "works throughout life after only one attunement," "empowers both the healer and the healee," "works on non-believers" and "flows automatically as much as necessary."

My Personal History of Reiki

I was one of the first students who received the attunement from Ms. Mitsui. I had been interested in the spiritual world and the Universal energy and went through the words and stories of Bahsharl, Shirley MacLaine and Sai Baba, and I found myself absorbed in healing techniques. I can list over 30 techniques I learned such as the *Nishino* Breathing Method, *Shinmeikan* Healing technique, SAS *Shinkiko*, *Genkyoku Qigong*, Crystal Healing, *Kihodo*

Healing, Hypnotic Qigong, Osteopathy, Energy Balancing technique, Astral Healing, SMC Silva Method, Natural *Hado-ho*, *Seiki-ho*, *Doki-ho*, Balance Therapy, Multi-dimension Body Work and so on. I met Ms. Mitsui when I was seeking a way to integrate all these techniques I had learned into my own healing method.

Although I was skeptical before the seminar, I found some changes in me after taking Levels I and II: feeling powerful, becoming healthy, tending to think positively and also the things around me started going smoothly. Above all, new ideas flashed across my mind: "Reiki includes everything I have learned so far." "Reiki might have a stupendous power within." "It encompasses, integrates and harmonizes itself, beyond the superficial knowledge of humanity."

Then I wanted to study Reiki thoroughly to confirm my instinct. Ms. Mitsui, however, was allowed to perform the attunements for only Levels I and II; she could not teach the higher levels. At that time in Japan, there was no teacher who could perform the attunements of Level III and more. I could have taken the seminar in the United States, but it required language skills because it was available only in English. She mentioned the possibility of inviting teachers over to Japan if we could gather enough students. (This did not happen though.)

Meanwhile, a German Reiki teacher, Frank Arjava Petter, and his Japanese wife, Chetna M. Kobayashi moved to Sapporo, in the northern area of Japan, and started a Reiki seminar in early 1993. He brought the know-how to teach the beginner level all the way to the teacher training course, and his know-how produced the first teacher of Western Reiki in Japan. Since then, the number of Reiki teachers keeps increasing, and it is estimated that there are approximately 50,000 people who learned from Western Reiki teachers as of January 1998. It is likely to increase more rapidly considering this stressful society we are living in.

Combining the East and West

When I found that I could not learn the higher Reiki levels from Ms. Mitsui, I came up with the idea that there might be someone in Japan who succeeded Usui Sensei in his tradition. I did everything I could to gather as much information as possible. Then at last, I found Ms. Kimiko Koyama, the eighty-six-year-old woman who was running the Usui Reiki Ryoho Gakkai as its sixth president. It was for members only, and had preserved its inherited tradition since its establishment. I soon enrolled in the Gakkai through one of the members and learned from Koyama Sensei. I was amazed at how different it was from the Western Reiki of Ms. Mitsui yet had been derived from the same root.

While practicing the Reiki-ho as taught by the two teachers, Mitsui Sensei and Koyama Sensei, I felt I needed to grasp the whole picture of Western Reiki. I wanted to be clear about whether Western Reiki had improved or degenerated from Dento Reiki, or become a totally different practice. I could see that receiving the second level from Mitsui Sensei was not enough for me to get a clear view about this.

Then I learned the whole course of Neo Reiki and became a Reiki Master at Manaso's school in Osaka. Neo Reiki is a unity of the Eastern and Western Reiki and proposed by Alpan who learned from Bhagwan Sensei in India. Additionally, I learned at diverse schools of Western Reiki all over Japan, including the one brought by Arjava Petter. Those experiences taught me that although they were all called by one name, "Western," there were some schools going in a different direction from that of the founder, Usui Sensei.

Around that time, many valuable materials regarding Dento Reiki and Usui Sensei as well as Western Reiki spontaneously came to me and gave me the answers to my questions. The Great Hanshin Earthquake (in January 1995) in Osaka and Kobe caused huge damage to the district we lived in. But we did not suffer much even though other houses turned into rubble. I felt that I was saved and given a mission I had to complete.

So again I studied the information I had collected, together with my experiences that had been aiming at the unity of Dento Reiki and Western Reiki. To be specific, I re-examined the Eastern and Western Reiki-ho as "Giho to heal mind and body" as well as "Giho to raise spirituality." As a result, I constructed Gendai Reiki Ho so that it avoided being too mysterious and prejudicial by leaving unknown/unproven things as they were, and with a motto to pass on its effectiveness through the actual proofs. Also, I tried to make the Giho as simple as possible so that they could be used easily on a daily basis.

Although I was doing it only for myself, I happened to teach two acupuncturists who were providing treatments using Ki. This gave me more chances to teach professional healers. The Gendai Reiki Ho system states, "Reiki is the way to health and happiness," and this was confirmed by the therapists. Consequently it encouraged me to establish the "Gendai Reiki Healing Association" to help spread it even more.

Then, I started to meet many people and groups who wanted more than Western Reiki. Some were looking for ways back to the original spirit of Usui Sensei's methods. Some Masters were trying to spread their unique theories on the integration of the East and West. Neo Reiki, which I have already mentioned, is also a new style of Reiki-ho uniting Western and Dento Reiki. Additionally, there were and are people who pursued Hayashi Sensei's ideas, which were the starting point of Western Reiki. Of course, we know that it was Takata Sensei who brought Reiki Ryoho from Hayashi Sensei to America. But I could find signs that he had already converted the "Usui method" into the "Hayashi method" even before he taught Takata Sensei. He seemed to try modernizing Reiki-ho based on his global perspective that stemmed from his medical knowledge and experience as a practical therapist.

The basic philosophy of Usui Reiki Ryoho is that the pathway to Anshin Ritsumei is entered through hand healing, and its ultimate goal is to attain the perfectly peaceful mind state. But it is rather difficult for people who are suffering from disharmonious conditions of the mind and body to concentrate on spiritual advancement. So Hayashi Sensei opened Hayashi Reiki Kenkyu-kai so that he could follow Usui Sensei's request to develop an easier method to scan for Hibiki or to be able to heal without the need to scan and treat Hibiki in order to make the practice of hand healing easier to practice so that everyone could do it. The Gakkai permitted him to study in his own way. Unfortunately the Gakkai changed its policy after Usui Sensei's death, and Hayashi Sensei had to leave to be able to work on Hayashi Reiki Kenkyu-kai. After the separation, he kept concentrating on the challenge given from Usui Sensei: "Giho for well-being of body and mind." His enthusiastic research was supposed to become the basis of Western Reiki.

There are some people who are trying to make Reiki-ho into a stepping stone to the power of esoteric Buddhism, because Mt. Kurama, where Usui Sensei had the revelation, had once had a connection to Tendai Buddhism. And, once you understand that Reiki-ho is "the pathway to health and happiness," it is quite natural that you would come across many different healing practices that follow the same path. As long as you are heading for "Love, Harmony and Healing," you can, through free will, walk on any path. There is no need to argue what is right or wrong; it is the seminar-takers themselves who must choose which way to go. I believe that many of the highly-motivated Reiki Masters/teachers will contribute to the unity of the East and West in various ways.

Reiki-ho, Now and in the Future

Although it was derived from Usui Reiki Ryoho, Western Reiki underwent unique development abroad. After growing up to be sophisticated and practical, it came back home. Dento Reiki, on the other hand, still emphasizes the fundamental consciousness to raise spirituality, and provides the techniques and exercises of self-dicipline.

Once the facets of both streams are shared, people will give up the easygoing idea that the whole ability is given only by the attunement. They will understand that the attunement just opens up the door; and that after entering the way of Reiki, they must develop and enhance their true ability on their own.

In Japan, in the last couple of years there have been two remarkable Reiki-related events worth noting: first, a Reiki teacher revealed the Reiki symbols, which, up until that time, had been kept secret and not allowed to be made common knowledge. Furthermore, he leaked information on how to give the attunement, with illustrations, in a magazine. Of course his actions provoked arguments, pro and con. Some Masters abroad, who did not understand the essence of Reiki, might have already published similarly controversial topics such as the disclosure of the Reiki symbols or the distant energy transmission. But it was the first time in Japan. Of course simply reproducing the symbols in a publication does not have a big influence on or change the essence of Reiki itself, but I do not think it is an appropriate action to take for a Reiki practitioner. As an example, it would be thoughtless behavior to open one's treasure box to people who are not interested in the box or its contents at all, especially when the treasure has been kept with great care and preciousness. How would you feel if someone took the *Go-shintai*[21] out of the shrine building you adore, and said, "Hey, look! This is in there?" I should avoid criticizing him without knowing his true intention. But I suppose he will bear the responsibility for what he has done.

The second noteworthy event was the foundation of the Reiki One Healing Association. "Reiki One" signified that Reiki would be unified as a single element under the philosophy of its founder, Usui Sensei. Its purpose in organizing was to provide the healthy promotion of Reiki beyond the principles and opinions of the separate lineages and schools. Anyone could join to share the common ideal that Reiki is the lesson of Love and Harmony.

Reiki One began in October 1997, and I served as an honorary advisor.

[21] 御神体 Go-shintai: the sacred object of worship in Shinto.

Many people from different schools registered, and it became a mainspring of the healthy promotion of Reiki, regularly publishing magazines, holding lecture meetings in Tokyo and Osaka, offering training sessions and holding the Koryu-kai mainly for the members in many places of Japan. (Reiki One Healing Kyokai completed its mission and finished in September 2000.)

Since 1996, I have held Gendai Reiki Koryu-kai every month in Ashiya City, where I live. Anyone who is interested in Reiki is accepted at this Koryu-kai. I am expecting that more activities of this kind will be held more often throughout Japan.

Let me forecast the Reiki-ho movement in Japan. There are five areas where I see changes occurring:

1) There will be more unification of the Eastern and Western Reiki-ho. And new, Reiki-based systems will make more progress. The spiritual advancement will be more emphasized than the healing techniques.
2) There will be fewer incomplete (half-done) seminars. There will be more chances available to learn Reiki-ho on a regular basis.
3) Reiki groups and instructors will have more chances for intercommunication to encourage their group activities.
4) There will be more opportunities for Reiki healing clinics to work in cooperation with modern medicine.
5) There will be more "true Reiki practitioners" who experience resonance with Reiki by performing healings, and who evolve in their daily life through the guidance of the hado of Love.

A word of caution, however. As Reiki receives more appreciation and notice from the public, there will also be a corresponding increase of less than professional teachers who are willing to jump on the bandwagon of the boom without a certain true awareness. When you are choosing a Reiki school, you must carefully choose the right one.

Chapter 4

Level I – Reiki Healing Basics

Background Knowledge

1) Reiki-ho is simple and profound.

You develop your healing ability using the hands and learn Reiki healing for yourself and others in Level I. Reiki smoothes the energy flow of your body and adjusts the balance. Consequently, your body and mind get relaxed and refreshed. The stress-free life with Reiki allows you to keep your health and beauty and stay young.

2) Reiki healing raises your natural healing ability and heals your body and mind.

Reiki does not oppose modern medical science nor does it replace it. While medicine approaches health from the physical perspective, Reiki revitalizes the life energy and raises the natural healing ability and immune system to heal the body and mind. How can it oppose medical science when it strengthens the life power, and adjusts the physical and mental balance? The root cause of disease should be cut off from both sides: Reiki and medical science.

3) Reiki healing is not a medical treatment.

It is illegal to provide a medical diagnosis or treatment without a medical license. It is also illegal for a practitioner to offer healing sessions using the names of acupuncture, moxibustion, massage and Judo therapy without possessing their licenses in Japan. You must avoid using confusing expressions as if you were giving those cures. It is hard to imagine any possible problems of that nature, as Reiki healing does not include any medicine or hard pressure on the body but only the light touch of the hand. You, however, must pay close attention to your words and deeds so that the clients do not misunderstand and think that you provide medical treatments. You also must not tell them that they do not need doctors or medication.

4) Reiki healing can be used with other techniques.

Reiki is effective enough by itself and also compatible with other techniques. The energy of Love is not exclusive. It unites and harmonizes with everything and generates a synergistic effect. If you have some religious belief, Reiki merges with its essence and enhances it with no contradiction or opposition.

5) The more you perform Reiki healing, the more powerful and exquisite it becomes.

Reiki is easy and simple; please use it every day. When Reiki healing becomes a natural part of your life to use in every situation, it means you benefit from a great treasure.

6) Basically it is better if you perform the healing longer.

Reiki is not a symptomatic treatment; it works on and heals the root of the disease. Therefore, it might take time to show a clear outcome. Of course, even a one-minute session can produce effects: the seasoned practitioner brings "the healing Light" with just a single touch or glance. But when the person does not want the healing, please do not impose it on him.

7) The sender and/or receiver might have an occasional reaction.

You might feel a sensation of pain or temperature change in your palms or an energy flow inside your body while healing. Sometimes the muscles twitch or the internal organs make noise. There is no need to worry about this. Just send Reiki until those sensations are gone. Move on to the next point when they are back to normal. It might happen sometime after the healing because Reiki keeps revitalizing the energy flow even after the healing. You are in the process of changing; just enjoy what is happening. And you do not need to worry if these things do not occur. You will feel more as your energy sensibility develops. Even if you do not feel anything at all, Reiki surely flows smoothly. This has been confirmed by Kirlian photography, which uses an electronic device that can record energy and has been measured by other electronic devices.

8) Reiki healing is an automatic control system of energy.

The sender is just a pathway of Reiki. Reiki automatically adjusts the energy flow as and where needed; it supplies the shortage and clears away the excess. Reiki also adjusts itself even to the energy level that is needed. The sender must not control it intentionally. Problems can occur when the sender controls something by his or her consciousness.

9) Both the sender and receiver get showered with Reiki when healing begins.

Healing begins when the sender puts his or her Reiki hands on a receiver and the necessary energy begins to flow into the receiver. At the same time, Reiki energy pours on both of them like a shower, and a swirl of Light surrounds them. The excess energy flows into the ground and they both get healed at the same time. The key for the smooth flow of Reiki is to just relax and feel the Love of the Universe.

How to Use Your Hands

Spread your palms lightly and put the fingers together naturally. The thumb can be a little apart. The energy becomes gentler and softer when they are wide open. Do not press with the hand; just use a light touch.

1) Using both hands

It is generally said that the left hand receives and the right hand sends. But in Reiki-ho, it is not necessary to choose which hand to use. Make full use of both hands. The whole body gets charged with Reiki from the point where the hand is placed. (It is also effective just holding the hand over, but put the hand on when possible because people feel comfortable with the warmth of hands.) Put your hands side-by-side to send Reiki to wide areas. Put one hand on the other one to send stronger Reiki.

2) Using one hand

It is sometimes easier to use only one hand on some parts of body. Use either hand in a natural and relaxed posture. For some areas, you can use the fingertips. It would be better to use both hands for paired organs, such as the lungs, kidneys and ears.

Healing Session

1) The room should be kept tidy, bright, quiet and well ventilated for a relaxing atmosphere.

When this is not available, purify the energy of the place with Reiki before starting. Even if the place is not ideal, do not be nervous. Have a blanket or bath towel ready as the receiver might feel cool as she begins to get relaxed. You can use healing music as needed.

2) Wash your hands before and after healing.

Your hands must be clean when you touch the receiver. Washing the hands is also an effective way to cleanse the negative vibration off your hands before a session. Rub your hands to warm them up after you wash them.

3) Both the healer and receiver should remove their watch.

The watch might be affected by the energy. The sender should take off things that might disturb the touch, such as rings or bracelets that will interfere, but can keep items such as glasses on. The receiver should take off things that tighten the body: a belt, a tie or unnecessary jewelry. Rings and earrings or other jewelry that isn't tight can be kept on as they get charged with good energy.

4) The receiver should be in a comfortable position, lying or sitting.

In either case, a relaxed posture is preferable. Do not fold the arms or legs. Try to release tension.

5) Hold the hands over the receiver when there are reasons that you cannot touch him or her.

When the healer cannot touch the person directly, due to a burn or skin disease, hold the hands about three to five centimeters above the body. Putting hands on the clothes or a blanket is as effective as holding hands over. When it is not appropriate for the sender to touch, but not a problem for the receiver himself, first ask the receiver to put his or her own hand(s) on his or her body, then the sender puts the hand(s) on the receiver's hand(s). You can put a towel or tissue over the receiver's face, if necessary.

6) Explain the post-healing changes.

The condition or the symptoms of the receiver sometimes seem to temporarily worsen after a healing. Some receivers get a fever, have increased excretion, eczema, pain and so on. The receiver does not need to worry about it because it is the process of being restored to health, called an improving reaction. (It is recommended that you explain it beforehand to avoid any concerns later.)

7) Reiki healing is performed in the following order.
   (1) Perform "Reiki Shower" (p. 125) to revitalize your energy
   (2) Relax the receiver and let him or her be in a comfortable posture
   (3) Aura cleansing
   (4) Put the hands on the basic 12 hand positions, for five minutes on each point (when your hands become more sensitive to feel *Hibiki* (p. 112) from the affected areas, you may follow the original healing way of Usui Reiki Ryoho)

(5) Put the hands on the areas as and where needed
(6) Aura cleansing after healing

Aura Cleansing

1) Aura cleansing must be performed before and after Reiki healing.

2) The aura cleansing before healing drains the excess energy, adjusts the aura and helps get back the energy balance. As your hand's energy sensitivity is developed, you will feel the areas with negative vibration.
   (1) The receiver lies down or sits on the floor or chair to be comfortable.
   (2) After raising both hands to connect to Reiki, the sender runs his or her hand(s) down or sweeps about 10 centimeters over the receiver's whole body. It is done downwards and/or left and right. The aura gets adjusted with the energy radiation from the sender's hand(s) and the stagnated excess energy flows off.

3) The aura cleansing after healing is crucial. As the energy of the whole body is purified by healing, the flow is accelerated. At the same time, if is in too delicate a condition to accept any kinds of hado the aura must be adjusted carefully so that the receiver will not be affected by any negative or harsh hado.
   The aura cleansing procedure is the same as the one before healing; lead and adjust the energy flow with gentle strokes. Let the receiver rest for a while (more than five minutes). When the receiver is still lying down, or in a relaxed, seated position, perform aura cleansing on one side of the body and do the other side after he gets up.

4) Aura cleansing can be performed for the sender by herself. It is unnecessary when a Reiki Shower or Jiko Joka Healing (Self-Purifying Healing) is performed.

The Basic 12 Hand Positions

1) Reiki healing for people is done to three parts of body: Head, Front and Back. And each part has four positions, which makes a total of 12 positions. They are called "the basic 12 hand positions for healing" (hereinafter: the basic positions).

2) They are H (head) 1 to 4, F (front) 1 to 4 and B (back) 1 to 4. Sections 3-5 offer a brief explanation of the effects of each position.

3) From the head positions, you can send energy into the front and back, and left and right sides of the brain (the center of the body). Reiki goes into the eyes, nose and the thyroid gland and gives relaxation and peace. Reiki also improves the immune system.
   (1) H-1 (Front of the face): Removes the pain in the eyes, nose, teeth and chin; Improves concentration and balance; Relieves stress; Raises the personality and spirituality
   (2) H-2 (Both sides of the face): Balances the pituitary gland and pineal gland; Adjusts the hormone levels in the brain; Removes headache; Balances the left brain and right brain; Relieves stress; Improves memory; Expands consciousness; Develops intuition
   (3) H-3 (Back of the head): The lower part of the brain, spine, cerebellum, occipital lobe; Develops language ability, eyesight and sense of color; Adjusts weight; Brings relaxation; Increases creativity; Releases fear; Expands insight and vision
   (4) H-4 (Throat): Revitalizes the circulation of the blood, lymph, throat, thyroid gland, blood pressure and metabolism; Increases confidence, peace, stability, joy and happiness; Increases creativity and communication abilities

4) From front positions (F), you can send energy to the thymus (the center of the immune system), internal organs, bladder and the genitals to adjust the balance.
   (1) F-1 (Thymus): Smooth the circulation of blood, heart, lungs and thymus gland; Gain confidence and adjust the emotional balance, release stress, increase receptivity to love, supreme bliss, stability and harmony
   (2) F-2 (Upper stomach): Liver, stomach, gallbladder, spleen, digestive system; Release from anxiety, fear and stress; Relaxation, peace, balance, tune to the energy in the higher dimension
   (3) F-3 (Tanden): Liver, pancreas, gallbladder, spleen, colon; Reduces stress, releases anxiety and dissatisfaction, increases confidence; Receptivity, confidence and strength
   (4) F-4 (Lower abdomen): Large and small intestines, the urinary bladder, the ovaries, womb, genitals, prostate gland, excretion; Heals sexual disorders; Releases anxiety, fear and tension; Brings more flexibility; Raises and widens consciousness

5) From the back positions (B), you can send the energy from the shoulders along the spine to the bottom of the womb through the kidneys and the adrenal gland.

(1) B-1 (Trapezius): Same as F-1. Add the following: heals any problematic conditions due to disorders in the neck, trapezius, the thoracic vertebrae, the lumbar vertebra, the spinal column and the nervous system; Provides relaxation

(2) B-2 (Middle of back): Same as F-2. Add the following: heals any problematic conditions due to disorders in the thoracic vertebrae, the spinal column and the nervous system; Releases tension

(3) B-3 (Lumbar): Same as F-3. Add the following: heals any problematic conditions due to disorders of the kidneys, the adrenal gland, the lumbar vertebra, the spinal column and the nervous system; Provides internal contentment

(4) B-4 (Sacrum): Same as F-4. Add the following: heals any problematic conditions due to disorders in the bones of the lower body such as the bottom of the spine, the coccyx and the pubis, as well as the nervous system

6) The whole procedure of the basic positions encourages the complete balanced recovery of the mind and body: the brain (the nervous system), the secreting gland system, respiratory system, digestive system, circulatory system, urinary system, sensory system, generation system, and muscles and bones.

The Basic 12 Positions (1) Head

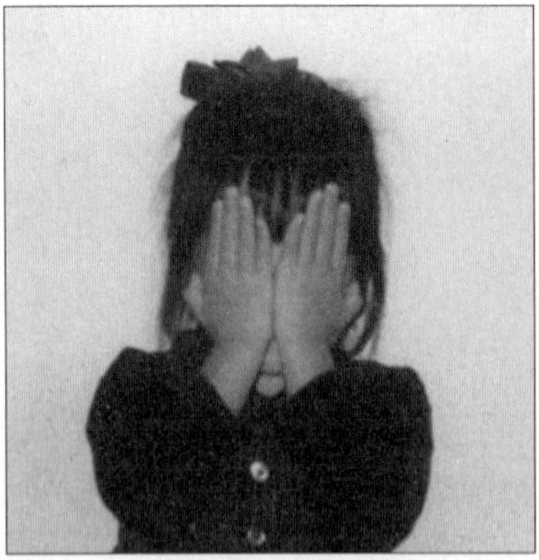

H-1 (Front of the face)

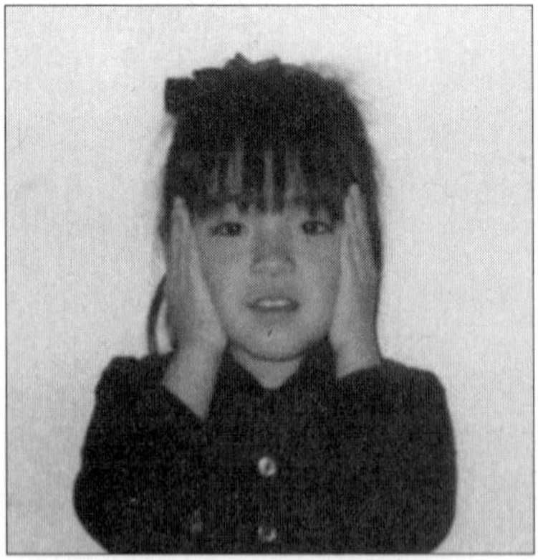

H-2 (Both sides of the face)

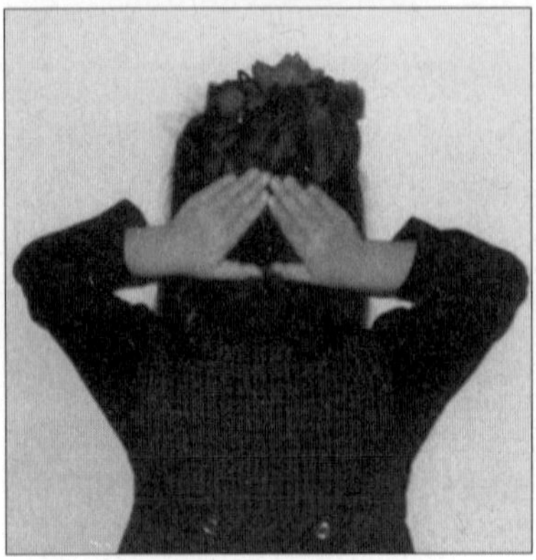

H-3 (Back of the head)

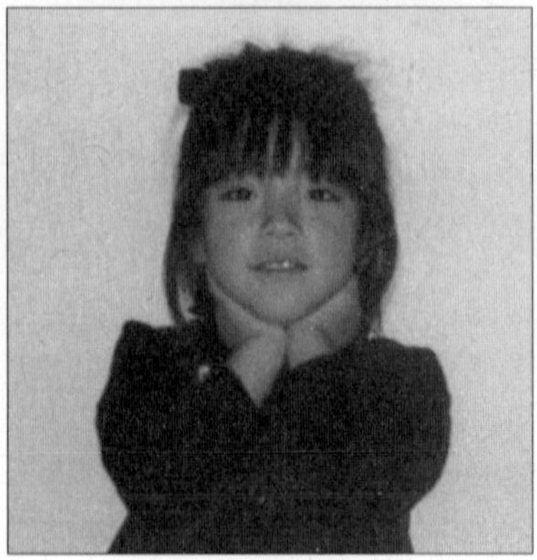

H-4 (Throat)

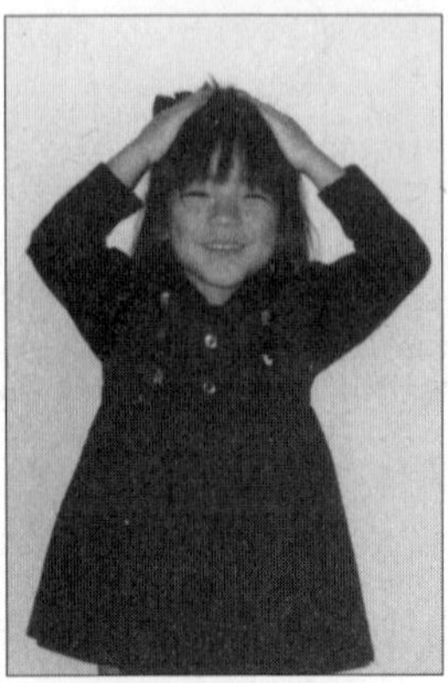

Alternative of H-2

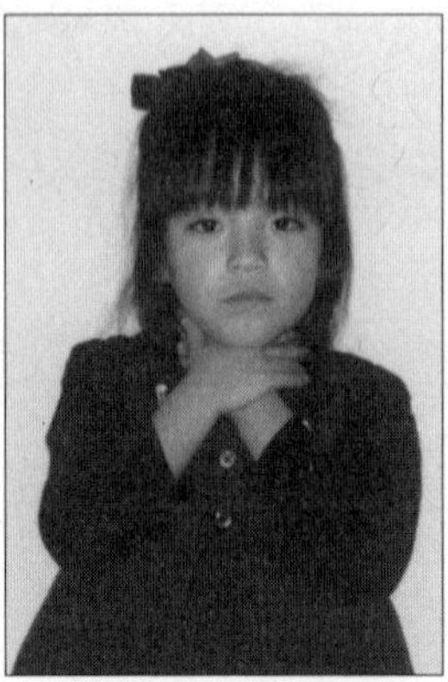

Alternative of H-4

Alternative of Head

The Basic 12 Positions (2) Front

F-1 (Thymus)

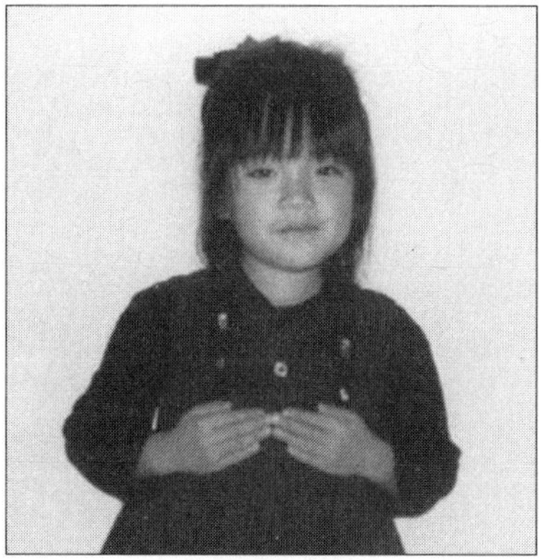

F-2 (Upper stomach)

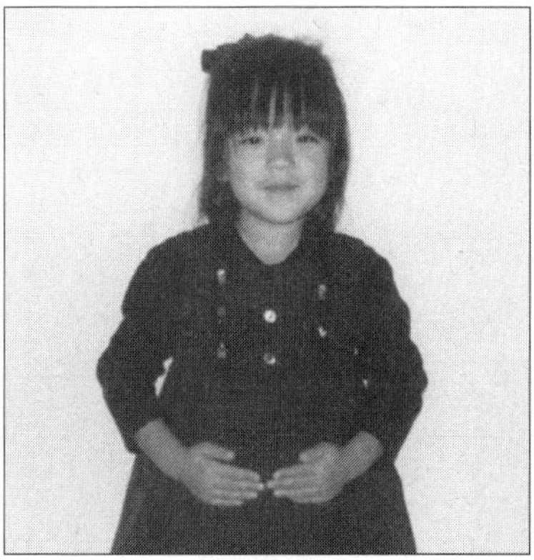

F-3 (Tanden)

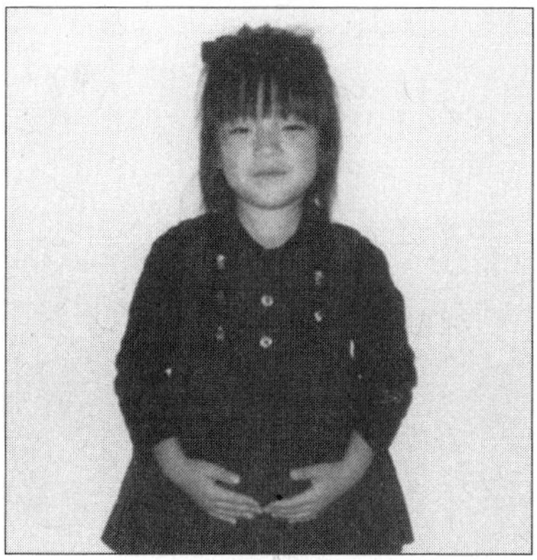

F-4 (Lower abdomen)

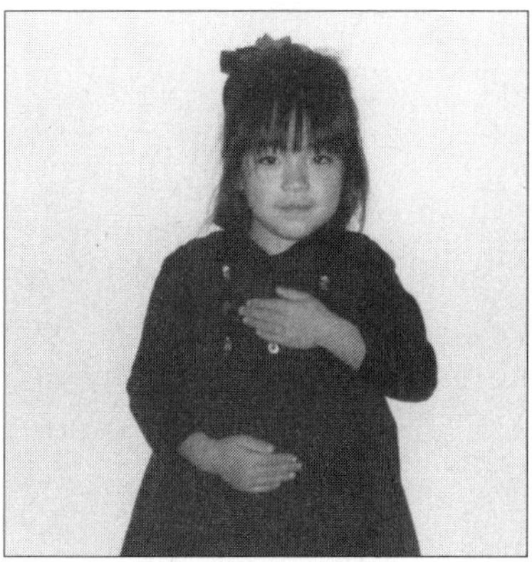

Alternative of Front (1)

Alternative of Front (2)

The Basic 12 Positions (3) Back

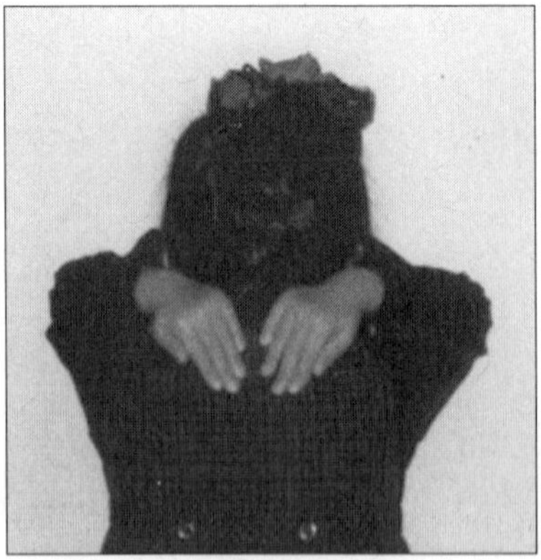

B-1 (Trapezius)

B-2 (Middle of back)

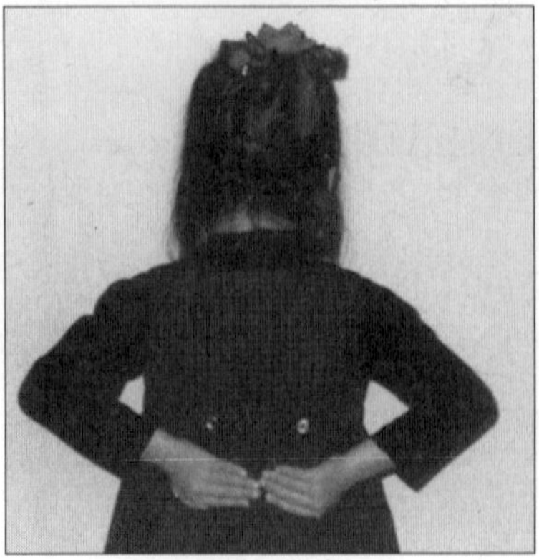

B-3 (Lumbar)

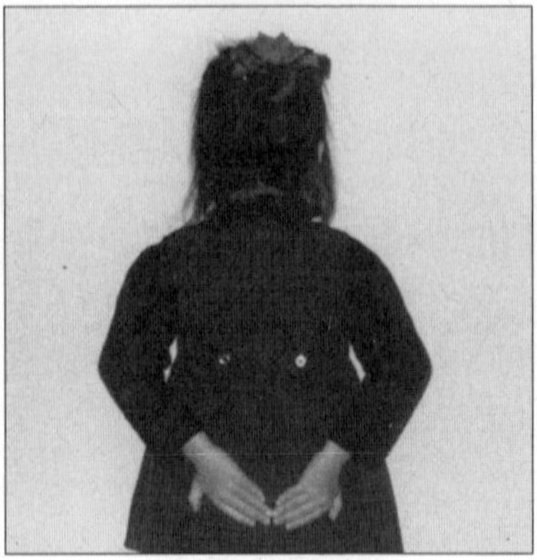

B-4 (Sacrum)

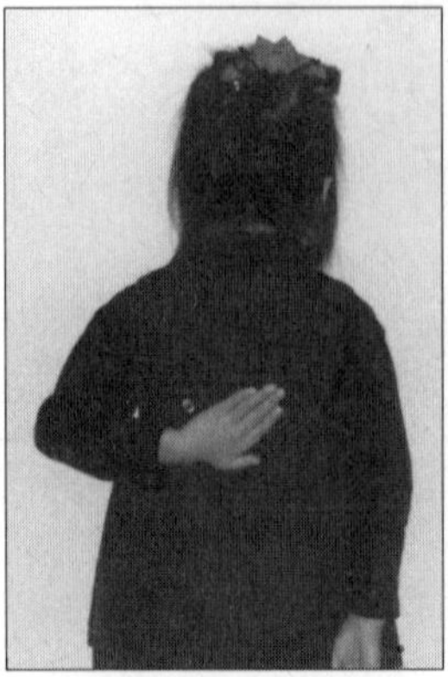

Alternative of B-2(1)

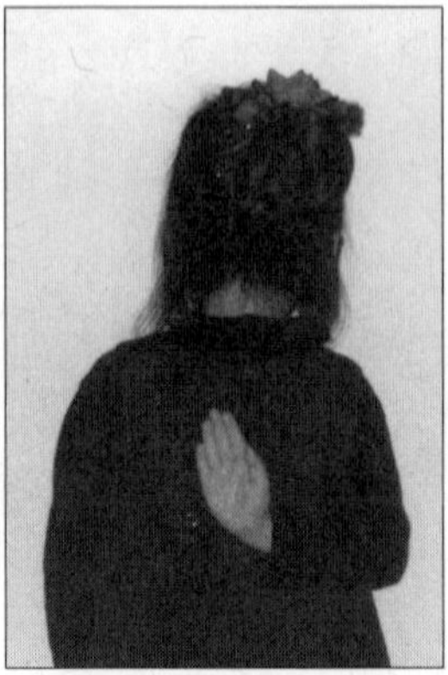

Alternative of B-2(2)

Alternative of Back

Reiki Healing for Yourself

1) Self-healing is performed by placing the hands on the basic positions respectively. When you cannot reach the points such as the ones on the back, put the hand(s) on the position close to them, intending that your hands are on the right position. Reiki surely goes to where you put your consciousness. You connect with Reiki the moment when you say, "Now I am going to do Reiki healing," or when you put your consciousness to Reiki or put the hand(s) on. This is because it's set up this way by the attunement.

2) The usual amount of time to send Reiki to each basic position for Level I practitioners is five minutes. It takes 60 minutes for all 12 positions. It has been proven by experience that this length of time shows the most effectiveness; however you can adjust the time depending on each person's skill. Only those who have just completed Level I should follow the basic rules.

3) After sending Reiki to the basic positions, you can put your hands on the disharmonious areas if you have any. When you do not have enough time, first heal the Head positions and then the disharmonious areas. In this case, there is no period of time set for each position; you usually finish when you feel some healing or recovery (the felt experience of some effect).

4) Reiki healing is very simple; feel free to perform it anytime and anywhere. Just a couple of minutes per each position still gives you a certain effect even when you have little time to spend. It is preferable to heal all 12 positions at one time in order to give you good balance; however, you can perform the healing separately at different times of a day, too. Doing this on a daily basis will help you heal your mind and body—releasing you from unnecessary tension and raising your consciousness.

Reiki Healing for Others

1) Originally the basic positions were developed for self-healing. But they are used for healing others as well nowadays. Put the hands on for five minutes per each position, following the suggestions listed above for self-healing.

2) When you want to mainly heal the disharmonious areas, first send Reiki to the Head section of the basic positions. We choose this area first because the brain is the center of the self-healing ability.

Reiki Healing for Animals and Plants

1) Animals

For animals such as dogs, cats, cows, horses and so on, start from the forehead and move onto the head positions and then the body. If you cannot touch them or they move too often, hold your hands over at a short distance away from them. For birds, gently hold them in both hands. You can gently hold their head or neck; they become comfortable and stable. You can hold the hands over the cage as well. For carp, gold fish, aquarium fish and so on, perform healing from the outside of the water tank or the pond. You can send Reiki into their food and water.

2) Plants

For trees, put the hands on the leaves, the trunks or the roots. For flowers, perform it like an aura cleansing: hold the hands over the stalks or the roots from both sides. Send Reiki to the seeds of plants and vegetables before planting or sowing. You can also do it to the soil and water.

Mr. Sohdai Tsujimi, who operates an accupuncture and moxibustion clinic in Kyoto was given a "tree of happiness" as a good luck present. But it died with too much water. His daily Reiki healing miraculously restored its life. But soon after that, it died from being left outside too long. He gave up and left it as it was during the whole winter. Then he tried Reiki healing next spring, and it revived again. Both he and his patients were amazed by its third life.

Cleansing and Injection of Energy

1) 邪気切り浄化法 *Jaki Kiri Joka-ho* (Cutting off and cleansing negative energies)

This technique drives away the negative and disharmonious hado attached to the body or to things, purifies them with Reiki energy and sends them positive energy.

Chop the air horizontally about 5 centimeters above the object with one hand, keeping the palm flat and swinging it like a karate chop. Reiki energy radiates from your palm. Then make a sudden stop of the hand movement when it has passed the object completely. Applying Jaki Kiri (cut off) three times changes the hado of almost all objects to a fine and harmonious one. (When you cut off, put your consciousness to the Tanden and hold your breath.) After you cleanse the object in this way, you can send it positive energy by giving a Reiki healing to the object.

2) Reiki for crystals and lucky charms
   (1) To cleanse small things like stones, jewelry or lucky charms, put the object on your palm and swing the other hand horizontally above it three times and do Jaki Kiri Joka-ho
   (2) Hold (or put) the hand over it and send Reiki energy
   (3) Repeat (1); cut the energy strongly three times
   (4) For larger objects, perform the above to a particular point of the object or imagine that it is small enough to be put on your hand

3) Reiki for the air in the room or the atmosphere of the place
   (1) Put one hand up towards the direction and cut off the negative energy of the four corners and the four walls counter-clockwise; then send Reiki with both hands
   (2) Do the same towards the ceiling and the floor
   (3) When it is not necessary to cut off the negative energy, just send Reiki facing your palm(s) to the four corners, walls, ceiling and floor
   4) Reiki for food and drink

   Send Reiki energy into the ingredients before cooking. You can also send Reiki before eating and drinking. Hold your hand(s) over or touch the container.

集団霊気 ***Shudan Reiki*** **(Group Reiki) and** 連続霊気 ***Renzoku Reiki*** **(Reiki Marathon)**

1) Group Reiki is a healing method given by several healers to one person at the same time. In a Reiki Marathon, two or more healers take turns to heal one receiver for a long period of time. Many examples have been reported in which cases of incurable diseases that had been given up on by modern medicine were healed by this method. Many Reiki schools explain the amazing outcomes such as these, especially those using Group Reiki, by saying that the effectiveness is equal to the square of the healers. In other words, the Reiki healing is four times as effective when performed by two healers and twenty-five times as effective when performed by five healers.

2) The hands are put on the basic positions and the disharmonious areas (mainly on a chief complaint).

3) If there are more healers offering help than can place their hands on the same location then some healers can put their hands on the shoulders or

back of the healers who have their hands on the receiver. They send "secondhand" Reiki, which is also as effective.

The Reiki Circle (*Reiki Mawashi*)

1) People make a circle, either hand in hand or by putting the right hand (palm down) on the left hand (palm up) of the people next to them. The left hand receives Reiki and your right hand sends it out to the person on the right. Reiki goes around from hand to hand by the speed of light. (Some people feel more energy when they hold over the hands than when they are actually touching hands.)

2) Non-practitioners can also feel Reiki when they are part of this circle. However, even if they do not feel it, Reiki circulation within the body is accelerated. If there are only two people present, they can do it facing each other.

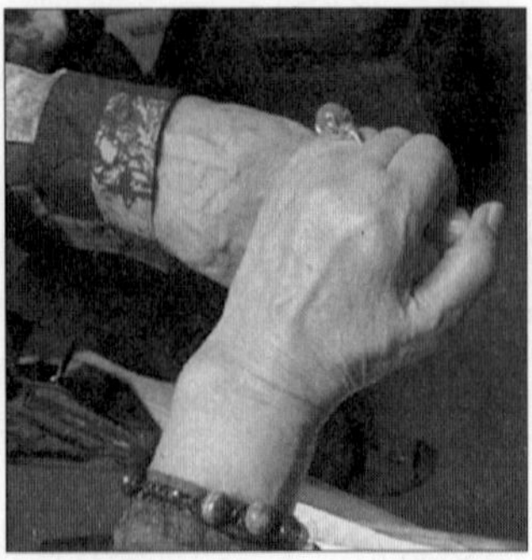

3) Another way to create an energy circle is to hold the middle finger of the person on the left with the left hand touching his or her fingertip with the ball of the thumb, thus circulating Reiki energy.

4) You can even do it by yourself: hold your right hand (palm down) over your left hand (palm up) in front of your body and calm your mind and just feel the energy. When you have developed skill with this method, you wil be able to meditate deeply this way.

Other Usages

1) You can send Reiki to everything you touch—bed, clothes, car and so on. (Try it as if you are cleansing and harmonizing the objects with Reiki from your palms.)

2) Send Reiki when you put money or a credit card back into your wallet, when you get in a car, when you take some medicine or a supplement, when you drink coffee or juice, when you eat, when you wear perfume and so on.

3) Only one moment of Reiki is enough. Just do it casually.

4) Ms. Noriko Hujimoto of Kenko Kaifuku (Regain your Health) Center in Suminoe-ku, Osaka used to do energy therapy with a gold bar. Now she does not use it anymore because Reiki from her fingertips is effective enough.

   Mr. Makoto Hurukawa of Hurukawa Acupuncture, Moxibustion and Shiatsu (finger pressure) Clinic in Kawachinagano City in Osaka says, "As you get skillful at Reiki-ho, any sort of treatment, such as acupuncture, massage, shatsu or other therapeutic sessions will also include Reiki energy, although the practitioner may not know Reiki is flowing."

After the Level I Seminar

1) Your pathway of Reiki is open and ready to heal yourself and others. However, you are still at the beginner's level, and you should try to upgrade the power gradually and steadily.

2) A most important point at this time is that you must keep the pathway clear for a smooth and full flow of Reiki before you try to strengthen the power.

3) For this purpose, I recommend that you take 21 days as the period of self-cleansing and perform self-healing on the basic positions. (The period of 21 days is recommended according to Usui Sensei's meditation and fasting time on Mt. Kurama.) The ideal is to do the whole body but just the Head part can be done if you do not have enough time. Put your hands on wherever you feel disharmony.

   In any case, perform healing for at least a few minutes in the 21 days. Of course you can perform healing on others. I also recommend taking extra water as your physical constitution changes gradually after the attunement.

4) Suggestions for upgrading your use of Reiki:
   (1) Use Reiki for anything in a casual manner: healing on people, animals, plants, food, accessories and places. In a coffee shop, for example, you can purify the water with Reiki from your palms and make it "the water of Life that activates your body." Read the manual again and again. You can ask questions of your Reiki Master right away if you come across anything that seems unclear.
   (2) Practice the "Self-purifying and Self-growth Giho" you learned at the seminar every day. They help you make your mind and body clear.

Chapter 5

Level II – Healing Beyond Time and Space

The Reiki Symbols and the Kotodamas

Reiki-ho adopts the symbols and Kotodamas to use the Universal energy. The healing technique using the symbols is called the "symbolized healing." You learn three symbols in Level II.

At the same time, you learn the Kotodama (mostly called mantra) corresponding to each Reiki symbol. There are some groups and schools that use the symbols but not the Kotodamas.

What Are the Reiki Symbols and the Kotodamas?

The Reiki symbols are shapes such as marks and letters, and are considered as "the antenna to tune into the Universal energy." It is said that energy comes out from some shapes or certain figures vibrating with some specific energies. For example, the pyramid and the Star of David are shapes that are well known as cosmic symbols that connect to the Universal energy.

Kotodamas are sacred voices (Shingon or mantras) and considered as vibrations that resonate with the Universal energy. The sacred voice of Om, the sound of a trumpet shell and clapping hands also bring about the resonance of hado.

The Reiki symbol and the Kotodama are essentially two different things. Dento Reiki has the symbols only, which are called 法 (*Ho*) or 秘法 (*Hi-ho*), and they do not have any Kotodamas.

Most of the Reiki groups employ the Kotodamas to enhance the effect of the symbols. (The Reiki symbols can be visualized or drawn with the eyes or tongue instead of the hands. Also you can visualize black symbols on the color purple behind your eyelids.)

First, you experience the high effectiveness of applying the Reiki symbols together with the Kotodamas. If you keep using them, you will find yourself getting the same results with the symbols only. Then, inevitably, you will no longer even need to use the symbols to get these results.

The Three Reiki Symbols

The first Symbol (S1) is called the power symbol and can be used in a variety of ways as it holds superior power. It is used by itself or with other symbols to amplify their power.

The second symbol (S2) is called the harmony symbol—exquisite and harmonious. It is always used together with the first symbol as it is said to be very delicate and fragile.

The third symbol (S3) is called the absentee symbol and works beyond time and space. It is effective when used together with the first and the second symbols in certain situations. This is the top symbol of Dento Reiki which I explain further on in the text.

The First Symbol (Power)

1) Meanings

(1) The distinctive feature is, in short, that the first symbol pinpoints the shape, matter and substance, and condenses and sends strong energy to it.

(2) The first symbol is related to the earth. The consciousness and the rhythm of the earth are programmed into the human body and constantly influence human life. For instance, the breathing rate of humans is 18 times per minute, which is the same as the rhythm of the ocean waves. Our internal system works in balance, constantly tuning to the rhythm of the earth.
18 x 2 = 36 Body temperature
36 x 2 = 72 Pulse
72 x 2 = 144 Systolic (maximum) blood pressure

(3) The above gives just a few examples among many. When you are out of balances with the rhythm of the earth, you get sick or experience misfortune. The first symbol matches the energy of the consciousness of the earth uses it to help everything return to its natural function.

2) How to Use the Symbol

(1) Draw the first symbol once with your finger in the air (or on the object), then repeat the first Kotodama three times and then send Reiki by putting your hands on (or holding them over).

(2) Repeat the Kotodama quietly enough so that only you can hear. Repeat it in your mind when you send Reiki energy to other people, or when you are with other people. Imagine that the Kotodama

spreads inside your body and echoes deeply inside your mind. Feel the Universal energy resonate with the Reiki symbol and the Kotodama. As you use it with pleasure, the energy becomes more and more powerful.

(3) When you are healing yourself or others, the symbol can be used with your hands on.

3) Examples

- To purify the energy of places or the environment
- To purify food and drink
- When coming back from hospitals or funerals
- For safe driving
- When you put money in your wallet
- To a credit card
- To a check or bill
- To change the weather
- For self-protection (Send the symbol to the front and back and right and left; or turn your body counterclockwise sending the symbol to the four directions)
- To motivate yourself (on the forehead)
- For better relationships
- To accomplish your dreams (no selfish desires)
- To things missing or left behind
- When you forget something (on your head)
- For business transactions and real estate dealings
- Before any business activity (to the area or direction)
- To a gift, greeting or business card
- To purify rooms and buildings (send the symbol to each corner)

S1 Symbolizes:	1. The Earth 2. Land 3. Power 4. Raising/Focusing Power 5. Visible things

Effects on Humans	1. S1 works on the body and revitalizes it 2. S1 activates chakras 1 and 2
Special Features	1. S1 connects to the Universal energy at the moment 2. S1 controls fate 3. S1 has great creativity 4. S1 raises the power of other symbols 5. S1 goes to a particular direction
Roles	1. S1 focuses on, sends energy to and activates all the substances on the earth 2. S1 awakens all the substances on the earth so that they realize their natural potential

The Second Symbol (Harmony)

1) Meanings

(1 The distinctive feature is to send the energy of balance and harmony, focusing on formless objectives like feelings or emotions.

(2) The second symbol relates to the moon. The moon greatly affects the human body. It also has a great influence on the whole earth; as is commonly known, the gravitational forces of the moon produce the ebb and flow of the tide. Seventy percent of the human body is water (body fluid), and it consists of the same constituents as the seawater; the body fluid is affected by the moon in the same way as the seawater and our feelings go up and down accordingly. The cycle of the moon is linked to that of women. These phenomena repeat, following the rhythm of nature, creating a world of balance and harmony.

(3) Synchronize the rhythm of the moon, and it will release any stress and free your blocked emotions. This symbol works on the conscious energy of the moon and regains the psychological and emotional balance while healing at a deep level by raising sensitivity and receptivity.

2) How to Use the Symbol

(1) Basically it is the same as the first symbol. Draw the second symbol once with your finger in the air (or on the object), repeat the second

Kotodama three times and then send Reiki, putting your hands on (or holding them over).

(2) After invoking the second symbol, it is necessary to use the first symbol.

3) Examples

- Use it on the part of your body that feels tense; it is effective on psychogenic pain, stiffness, fatigue, neurosis and stress
- To ease mental confusion, calm anger, heal sorrow, release blocked emotions and to refresh yourself
- Before meeting people, in negotiations and interviews; to a place, circumstance and situation; to bring peace and harmony to relationships
- To forgive yourself and others
- To release old negative emotions that are attached to you
- To get the guidance from the Universe to raise your spirituality and to return to what you are
- To change negative habits, behaviors and mental attitudes into positive ones
- For self-growth, by putting your hands on both sides of your head or front and back and send Reiki
- For self-achievement (Put your right hand on the front [the forehead] and the left hand on the back of your head)

S2 Symbolizes:	1. The Moon 2. Water 3. Yin 4. Feelings and emotions 5. The Ether 6. Harmony 7. Invisible things
Effects on Human	1. S2 works on the feelings and harmonizes them. 2. S2 activates chakras 3 and 4

Special Features	1. S2 adjusts the balance of psychological and emotional energy 2. S2 helps self-growth 3. Wish fulfillment 4. Fragility
Roles	1. S2 returns the unbalanced emotions back to where they should be and harmonizes them 2. S2 improves the egoistic personality and leads one back to one's "true-self" granted by the Universe 3. S2 is from the Sanskrit character that means "release and salvation from all the sufferings"

The Third Symbol (Absentee)

1) Meanings

(1) The distinctive feature of this symbol is to send Reiki energy that is focused on the center of the objective beyond time and space like a time machine.

(2) The third symbol is related to the sun. We greatly benefit from the sun; as we know, the four seasons, day and night, light and shade all come from the sun. The earth, and needless to say, humanity could not survive a single day without the sun. It is the very root of all existence.

(3) The third symbol approaches the conscious energy of the sun, and it allows us to go beyond everything. It does not mean to escape but rather to accept, adopt and heal its objective. The power reaches the center of the object beyond time and space and brings transcendence and change. This symbol is mainly used for distant healing, purifying karma and trauma and creating a bright future.

(4) The third symbol is said to mean, "I become one with God." My interpretation from its Kotodama is, "The root of every being is the right consciousness." The true consciousness is the resonance (unity) of the Great Universe and the little universe (human). Both interpretations are quite identical.

(5) This symbol is used to connect to the objective of distant healing in Level II. After acquiring proficiency in Level III, the third symbol,

which is the most important symbol in Dento Reiki, allows you to provide healing without the first and second symbols.

2) How to Use the Symbol

(1) Draw the third symbol once with your finger in the air (or near the object), then repeat the third Kotodama three times and then send Reiki by putting your hands on (or holding them over).

(2) If the object of distant healing is pure substance, send the third and the first symbol and then Reiki. If it contains something emotional, send the third, second and first symbols and then Reiki. You can draw all of the symbols (the third, second and first) and send Reiki to any objectives.

3) Examples

- The third symbol can be used for healing beyond time and space on any substance and any situation. The effect on the emotions and mentality is supposed to be deeper than that of the second symbol. Try and make use of it in any situation.
- Other energy-workers, such as Qigong practitioners, can send the energies of their own methods with the third symbol. However, it is not recommended to do so when those methods or treatments require one's consciousness to control something.
- To improve the genetic constitution, send Light (S3) and perform Reiki healing onto genes, focusing on the DNA.
- Distant healing is not always to the places far from you. For example, you can use it as follows:
  (1) Send Reiki to your child studying upstairs when you are downstairs
  (2) Send Reiki from the dining room to your spouse who is tired and sleeping in the living room
  (3) Send Reiki from your house to the building, room or facility where an occasion is being celebrated
  (4) Send Reiki to the image of yourself standing in front of you
  (5) Send Reiki to the picture of a person or a piece of paper with his name on it
- You can distant-heal yourself with the third symbol. Choose three parts of your body and put your hands on the first part for five minutes, declaring "Head." Then move your hands to the second part, saying "Front" and to the third, saying "Back." If you have time, you may put hands on all 12 hand positions.

S3 Symbolizes:	1. The Sun 2. Fire 3. Yang 4. Light 5. Astral Form 6. Spirit 7. Transcendence
Effects on Human	1. S3 works on the spirit, giving it calmness and peace 2. S3 activates chakras 5 and 6
Special Features	1. Distant healing beyond time and space 2. S3 removes bad karma and trauma 3. S3 connects with every substance and situation 4. S3 can be used together with other symbols.
Roles	1. S3 works beyond time and space and connects the consciousness to distant places, past and future, to create balance and harmony. 2. S3 purifies and removes bad karma and heals trauma. 3. S3 connects to the center of the object and lets it transcend and transform.

Distant Healing

Distant healing is a technique to send Reiki energy at a distance.

1) You can use a picture or drawing.
   (1) Prepare a picture of the person (or a drawing with the name).
   (2) Place it on a table and repeat the person's name three times.
   (3) Send the third symbol (the second and first symbols when necessary) to the middle of the forehead of the person.
   (4) Send Reiki from head to toe and aura-cleanse to finish.
   (5) You can make your body the medium to send Reiki to the receiver: after (3), put your hands on your own basic 12 positions (or three

parts of your body that you have chosen beforehand).

2) Using a life size-image
   (1) Imagine a life-size energy body of the person in front of you.
   (2) Send the third symbol (the second and first if necessary) to the forehead of the image.
   (3) Send Reiki and aura-cleanse to finish.
3) Using a mini-sized image
   (1) Put a mini-sized image of the person between your hands and send Reiki to its entire image. (You can also imagine a part of the person's body if it is easier)
   (2) Your hands can be held either top and bottom or right and left of the image.
   (3) Follow above steps (2) and (3).

Healing the Past

This technique is to heal trauma in the past, and cleanse and remove karma.

1) Remove bad karma and trauma

   Suppose you had hurt someone in the past without thinking. If you blame yourself every time you remember that experience, it would be a kind of karma. Suppose you were injured in the past. Even if the physical pain is already cured, still you can suffer from psychological pressure. This would be a kind of (psychic) trauma. Send Reiki with the symbols to heal those pains and negative emotions.

   (1) Put your mind on the unsolved problems (situation, person, place, etc.) and send the third, second and first symbols respectively in the air.
   (2) Hold your hands over a piece of paper with the name of the person and you, and repeat both names three times. Remember the details of the problem as much as possible.
   (3) Send Reiki and feel that the spirits of both that person and you unite in the vibration of Reiki. Feel deep inside you that both spirits have already become one in harmony with the Universe.
   (4) Aura-cleanse the paper and do Gassho. Imagine that the person and you forgive each other now. Send your sincere appreciation and joy for the forgiveness to the Universe.
   (5) When the object is not a person, create an image of the object; if you cannot describe it or draw it, send Reiki to the image for the time and the place it occurred
2) Re-experiencing a joyful memory

The memories of joy and success always make your heart beat faster. So do the feelings of victory after long-lasting hardships. Experiencing those memories again secretes hormones that create pleasant feelings inside the brain and raises your motivation. As long as you are not absorbed by it, you can use those memories to cheer you up.

(1) Repeat the pleasant memory three times (for example, winning a marathon, passing an exam.)
(2) Close your eyes and remember the details as clearly as possible.
(3) Towards the image, draw the third, second and first symbols and send Reiki energy. (You can hold one hand over the image or put it between your hands.)
(4) Do Aura cleansing and Gassho. Send your sincere appreciation to the Universe.

Healing the Future

This technique is to send the Light of Reiki to yourself and the situations you hope for in the future.

1) Give the Light and blessing to yourself in the future.

Imagine that you are performing in the best and most relaxing condition at all your important events: business, presentations, games and so on. Send the Light and blessing towards the image.

(1) On a piece of paper, write down your name, the time and place of the event and how you hope to be there, and repeat the time and date three times, focusing on the paper
(2) Close your eyes and imagine how the situation should be in the future as clearly as possible
(3) Draw the third, second and first symbols with your finger on the paper and send Reiki
(4) Do aura cleansing and Gassho; Send your sincere appreciation to the Universe

2) Give the Light and blessing to others in the future.

For the person's important event such as an examination, presentation, family trip and so on, imagine the person is there in the best condition and send the Light and blessing towards the image. This process is the same as above #1). You can also do it without writing on paper as below:

(1) Repeat the name of the person three times
(2) Close your eyes and imagine how the situation should be in the

future as clearly as possible
(3) Draw the symbols with your finger towards the situation (or the person) and send Reiki.
(4) Do aura cleansing and Gassho; send your sincere appreciation to the Universe.

The Reiki Box

1) This technique is for more than two wishes to be granted at the same time. However, you must not employ a Reiki Box to satisfy your egoistic or selfish desires.
2) Prepare a suitable box (nonmetallic). Write or draw one wish on one piece of paper.
3) Imagine that the wish is granted. Draw the third, second and first symbols with your finger on each paper with their Kotodamas (three times each). Put the paper in the box and keep it where no one can see it.
4) Draw the third, second and first symbols towards the box with their Kotodamas (three times each) and send Reiki every day. It would be more powerful if you take the sheet(s) out of the box and give them Reiki every day.

The De-programming Technique (To dismiss self-limitation)

It is said that this method releases you from brainwashing and mind control; it works on the subconscious mind to help it stop acting out of unfavorable habits and attitudes.

1) Do aura cleansing. Put one hand on the back of the person's head. Over the hand on the person's head, draw the third, second and first symbols with their accompanying Kotodamas using the other hand.
2) Put the other hand on the person's forehead (the first hand is still on the back of the head) and feel the Light filling within you and then that it is flowing into the receiver. Imagine both the receiver and you are filled with the Light.
3) Repeat the affirmation (the positive words the receiver is wishing to empower) three times in your mind. Do an aura cleanse to finish.

After the Level II Seminar

1) The attunements of Level II enhance the energy flow inside you. Furthermore, more varied uses of Reiki are available by using the three symbols:

(1) Healing and cleansing at the substantial and physical levels
(2) Healing and cleansing at the spiritual and subconscious levels
(3) Healing and cleansing the past and future at a distance

2) What you should do now:

(1) First try as many Giho with the Reiki symbols as possible. especially since the healing (for self and others) has become much easier to do as the time required is shortened to two and a half minutes per each basic position (30 minutes to finish all 12 positions). You can shorten the time more by using the symbols.
(2) Second, choose a favorite and comfortable Giho for yourself from among those you have tried. You do not necessarily need to be versed in all of them. You may give them your own arrangements for your personal use so that you can build up your own practice style.
(3) In order to utilize Reiki in your daily life, arrange Giho in a simpler way. Keep practicing until you can experience enough of the effect by using the symbols without the Kotodamas.
(4) Please keep practicing as you are raising your consciousness and preparing for Level III, the highest level of Reiki-ho. For this purpose, exercise the Self-purifying and Self-growth Gihos that I recommended at the end of the Level I and Level II seminars every day to develop your energy sensing abilities of the hands, the intuition, the third eye and so on.

Chapter 6

Level III – Raise Consciousness by the Light of Reiki

Make the Best Use of What You Have Learned

It is truly to be blessed to reach the highest level, Level III, of Reiki-ho. Level III is called Shinpi-den in Dento Reiki, and it was extremely difficult to be accepted to this level.

Even though Usui Sensei's open attunements to the general public contributed to the popularization of Reiki, he seldom allowed his students to take the Shinpi-den lesson. It is confirmed that he taught Shinpi-den to only 21 out of 2,000 students.

Takata Sensei, who practiced Reiki healing sessions in Hawaii, did not pass on Level III to any of her students for about forty years, until late in her life.

Level III is now open to everybody. I suppose it is because the Intelligence of the higher dimension acknowledged the need and broke the seal to raise human awareness. The life or death of the earth depends on the advancement of our spirituality. Although Level III is open to the public, it is not for everyone who wants it. You must be an appropriate person and be ready for it. I believe that you are granted this chance to learn Level III because you have reached a certain level, and it is your mission from the Universe.

The accomplishment of Level III is the final goal of Reiki-ho; Level I and II are only the preliminaries for it. Just reaching this "goal," however, does not mean that you are finished. It means you are on the starting line where you only "know" that the purpose of life is to attain Anshin Ritsumei. In other words, you are like Usui Sensei before the true awakening. The actual course to Anshin Ritsumei has just begun. When Usui Sensei was alive, being chosen as Shinpi-den practitioners designated that those Gakkai members were allowed to take the person-to-person lecture directly from him on how to attain Anshin Ritsumei. It did not mean they had obtained it.

Level III gives you the fourth symbol as the effective tool that can be used for spiritual advancement. Although Dento Reiki does not have this symbol, (Usui Sensei did not have it) it is called the Usui Symbol or Master Symbol in Western Reiki schools and known as the symbol that leads us to Universal consciousness and gives us the Light. Since then a great many Western practitioners have used it as the sacred symbol. Consequently it produces the heightened effect that leads us straight to spiritual development.

The Fourth Symbol (Master Symbol)

1) Meanings

(1) This is the highest symbol of Western Reiki. It connects one with the Universal consciousness and brings this Light to our consciousness. Though Dento Reiki does not have this symbol, Gendai Reiki Ho employs the West's appreciation and usage of the fourth symbol for spiritual development as it provides positive group-consciousness for Western practitioners.

(2) Some groups might have additional symbols but those are not part of traditional Reiki-ho. (There are possibilities that some people might receive other symbols by a revelation according to their consciousness. I believe that they can receive and use them only for their own benefit and practice.)

(3) The fourth symbol is considered very sacred overseas; some groups even teach that it invites God. And they add more meanings to it—for example, the guiding symbol that leads to spiritual awakening.

(4) Basically, receiving the fourth symbol means you obtain the energy of the higher dimension, which enables you to pass on Level I, II and III to people who want to learn Reiki-ho. This is one of the reasons why it is called Master Symbol. (You learn how to pass on Reiki energy in detail in Level IV, and it is necessary to confirm that you have kept truly clear energy.)

(5) There is an idea that we reincarnate in this world to move on to the higher level through the necessary learning experiences, and that we come back here over and over again until we complete the lessons. What we should learn in this life depends on the individual because each person has a different past, but one thing in common is that we must let go of all illusions and the ego and reach Satori, spiritual enlightenment. When we get to this stage, we go beyond the level of "human" and enter into the dimension of eternal peace, calmness and supreme bliss; in other words, our spirits become one with the Great Universe. Many spiritual leaders who wanted to reach this level endured rigorous trainings. They call it *Gedatsu* (enlightenment, liberation). Those who aspire to enlightenment believe that the fourth symbol liberates them from the cycle of life.

(6) On the other hand, some people think that there is no reincarnation at all and we have only one life. The fourth symbol leads those people as well, to become aware of the meaning of self-existence and live a valuable life.

(7) Until you reach your goal or as long as you are striving for it, the fourth symbol keeps guiding and supporting you by providing the vision of the brilliant Self standing on the finish line.

2) How to Use the Fourth Symbol

(1) Draw the fourth symbol once with your finger in the air (or on the object), repeat the fourth Kotodama three times and then send Reiki by putting your hands on (or holding them over).

(2) Use the fourth symbol before other symbols. The Light and hado from the Universe will be added to the following symbols, and they will be finer and more harmonious. Therefore it is important to use the fourth symbol before other symbols.

For example, to purify a ring, send the fourth symbol and then the first symbol. When you cleanse something at home from a distance, send the fourth, third and first symbols. If those things contain any psychological or emotional aspects, send the fourth, third, second and first symbols respectively.

3) Examples

- The fourth symbol can be used before self-cleansing meditation, and breathing techniques to make them more effective. You can also send it after those practices to retain their effects.
- Start Reiki sessions by sending the fourth symbol and the Kotodama. You can also send the fourth symbol and let the Kotodama resonate inside you after the session.
- The fourth symbol can be used before and after Qigong practice, healing techniques, energy work and body work. Also it is effective to send the fourth symbol and be surrounded by the energy of the Light before starting activities in your daily life: playing musical instruments, writing an essay or poem, before business talks or before making important decisions. You can also purify with the fourth symbol afterwards.
- Use the fourth symbol and its Kotodama whenever and wherever you confront negative emotions or unpleasantness. And feel that you are with your Higher-Self. Accept what is happening to you and be thankful for it; this is helping your self-growth. (Do not escape but just purify them, or the same thing will happen over and over again.)

- Use the fourth symbol and the Kotodama when you have problems you cannot solve in spite of making a great effort. Then leave the solution to the Universe. The most appropriate answer will be given when needed.
- Send the fourth symbol and the Kotodama to the Universe for desperate situations.
- On page 66 I wrote that the third symbol allows the Level III practitioner to provide all the healing energies needed. However, if you have even a little uncertainty, use all the symbols because the effectiveness of your healing energy depends on your confidence. The fourth symbol must be used for your spiritual development; to upgrade the energy level and to create a peaceful state of mind.

S4 Symbolizes:	1. The whole Universe 2. God 3. The energy body 4. Wind 5. The sky 6. Komyo 7. Satori
Effects on Human	1. Healing 2. Relaxation 3. Balance 4. Activates chakra 7
Special Features	1. The supreme symbol 2. S4 brings the Light into darkness and heals 3. S4 brings the Light to other symbols
Roles	1. S4 brings the guidance from the higher dimension, allows one to know the meaning of life and one's mission and to live a full life 2. Hado of Komyo brought by this symbol permeates into the user's body to give great awareness

Receive Guidance from the Higher-Self All Day

Start and finish every day by sending the fourth symbol and the Kotodama. Make it your daily routine, and you can get guidance from the Higher-Self all day long.

1) When you get up in the morning, draw the fourth symbol in the air and repeat the Kotodama. Gassho and say the affirmation, feeling the Light and vibration from the Universe: "I will do appropriately what I should do by the guidance and healing of the Higher-Self all day today. I am improving and harmonizing in many ways." (You can choose your favorite affirmations following your intuition.)
2) When you go to sleep at the end of the day, draw the fourth symbol in the air and repeat the Kotodama.

   Gassho and say the affirmation, feeling the Light and vibration from the Universe: "I am thankful for being with the guidance and healing of the Higher-Self all day today. I am improving and harmonizing in many ways."
3 After saying the affirmations, you can send out positive prayer/vibration such as: "May the whole Universe be in peace. May all humans be in happiness. May all people be blessed" (only when you feel comfortable to do so).

Connect to a Higher Dimension and Receive Guidance

The first Giho is to use the fourth symbol to connect to the vibration of the spiritual leaders who have reached the higher stages: the benevolence of Buddha, the love of Jesus Christ, the wisdom of Einstein, the spirituality of Gandhi, the mercy of Mother Teresa and so on. The second Giho is to connect to your Higher-Self. In either situation, just a superficial curiosity cannot raise your vibration.

1) Connect with the spiritual leaders
   (1) Gassho, be calm, relax and be receptive.
   (2) Draw the fourth symbol in the air and repeat the Kotodama three times and hold up your arms in the front of your body. Feel that you are connected with the Universe.
   (3) Close your eyes and be conscious of the person and the subject you wish to explore. (You can write it on a piece of paper in advance.) When you do not have any particular subject or question, just close your eyes and imagine the person.
   (4) Gassho and feel that the whole of you melts into the conscious-

ness of the Universe. Feel that the Universe and you are completely united and let the consciousness of the person join you. Now feel that the Universe, the person and you are One.

(5) When the vibration of the spiritual leader touches you, holds you and starts resonating with you, tell that being of your concerns. If you have no words, just feel the sensation. Just feel this spiritual presence without doubt, denial or fear.

(6) The answer might be given in your dreams or as a flash in your mind some other day. You might find it during conversation with someone or in a book. If you do not find it, the subject is probably not necessary for you or it is not the right time.

(7) Gassho and finish calmly with gratitude.

2) Connect with the Higher-Self.

(1) Gassho. Calm your mind, relax and be receptive.

(2) Draw the fourth symbol in the air and repeat the Kotodama three times and hold up your arms in front of your body. Feel the connection with the Universe.

(3) Close your eyes and put the palm of your dominant hand on your heart. Breath slowly and say "My dear Higher-Self" or "My dear soul" (in any way you want) and calm your mind to be able to listen to the delicate feelings inside yourself.

(4) Repeat (3) with the other hand on the heart.

(5) You will feel the different sensations from each hand. (Even if you do not feel anything at first, you will soon feel something as you try.) What you feel depends on each person and the timing; it is not always the same. It could be, for example, "a subtle sensation deep inside," "an indescribable peace of mind" or "a touch of warmth." When you feel something like comfort, relief, warmth, vibration or silence and so on, put the hand that you got the feeling with on the chest again. (If you feel something with both hands or nothing with either hand, put the non-dominant hand on the chest.)

(6) Keep your mind calm and feel the interaction between your Higher-Self and your palm. The Light of the higher dimension permeating from your palm cleanses everything blocking the brightness of your Higher-Self: negative emotions, memories, trauma and bad karma.

You do not need to control your breathing; just breathe naturally. Put your consciousness lightly on the hand on the chest and keep feeling the sensation from inside. (But do not concentrate too much; be natural. Relax and enjoy the fine and faint signals. It is okay if you do not feel anything. You will be able to feel something soon.)

(7) Gassho and finish calmly with gratitude.

The Higher Light Purifies and Helps You Grow Through Meditation

As you are already aware, Level III is not just a step to simply learning many techniques. Level III is the great step to true self-actualization by 1) the fourth symbol, which is the highest symbol; it connects you to Universal Consciousness and brings in the Light, 2) the practice of healing which purifies your energy and protects you and 3) Self-purifying and Self-growth Giho which align you ever more completely with the higher resonance of Reiki. The constant guidance from the higher dimension through the above three practices expands your consciousness and spiritual awareness, enhances your intuition and imagination and gives you a better understanding of the meaning of self-existence, and you are also guided in everyday activities as well as what you are to do with your life.

1) There are several steps toward self-actualization.
   (1) Know yourself (self-recognition).
   (2) Accept yourself as you are (self-acceptance).
   (3) Change yourself into what you are meant to be (self-transformation).
   (4) Resonate with the Universe and live a creative life (self-actualization).
2) As we are going through these steps in daily life, we must:
   (1) Purify and cleanse the trauma and negative imprints piling up deep in our subconscious mind and the negative hado caused by our past emotions and actions.
   (2) Live life without producing new negativity any more.

   Some Giho such as "Self-cleansing with the Light" and "Reiki Meditation" are helpful in solving these problems. Some of them are introduced in Part III, "Self-purifying and Self-growth Giho." To live without negative hado, you must train yourself to raise your consciousness. There is no other way. Usui Sensei's Go-kai tells you how to practice on a daily basis.

Chapter 7

Level IV – Transmit Reiki Appropriately as an Instructor

Qualifications and Roles

Level IV is the last step in learning Reiki-ho. As you already reached the highest energy in Level III, there is no energy transmission included. (In Gendai Reiki Ho, you take the Integrated Attunement with all four symbols in Level IV.)

You learn how to teach correctly and spread Reiki-ho to many people. It is a training course for Reiki instructors rather than extra steps for learners. Those who have completed this course with their ability approved are called Reiki Masters or Reiki teachers (hereinafter Reiki Master).

The more precise definitions of the qualifications for Reiki Masters are:

1) They completed Levels I, II, III and IV (or Master course).
2) They are sending clear Reiki energy and are able to perform the attunements correctly.
3) They are able to explain the meaning of the Reiki symbols and Kotodamas, teach how to use them and provide the attunements.
4) They are able to instruct on the true nature of Reiki and its overall usage.

A long time is spent in learning how to give the attunement of Reiki energy since it is the essence of Reiki-ho. As Koyama Sensei of the Usui Reiki Ryoho Gakkai repeated to its members, "Pass on the right Reiki"; the energy transmission is, of course, crucial. But she did not mean the attunement technique was the only thing you had to be proficient in.

In respecting the prescribed forms, the most important thing is the energy itself. As I point out in Questions & Answers (Part 2), you cannot pass on clear Reiki energy if you only focus on the token techniques without Kokoro.

I sincerely hope that all who want to become Reiki Masters learn not only the attunement techniques or Reiki usages. It is also necessary to understand Usui Sensei's spirit as the founder of Usui Reiki Ryoho and the ultimate usage of Reiki-ho so that you convey it in the right way.

Keep Practicing and Keep Teaching

The spiritual leader who reaches Satori is called "Master" but a Reiki Master does not necessarily need to be on that level. You can understand the term Reiki Master as a person who mastered Reiki-ho, who is well experienced and qualified to teach Reiki-ho. Of course, Reiki Masters should train themselves to become spiritually awakened in the early stages with the constant support of the Universe.

One religious teaching says, "If you preach to people in the wrong way, your soul will not be saved until all those people are saved." Although Reiki-ho is not a religion, Reiki Masters are required to keep a sincere and modest attitude because they connect to the source energy of the Universe and work on the super-consciousness of people. So, it does not make any sense if Reiki Masters do not live their daily lives according to what they teach. They must practice a peaceful way of life in the resonance with the hado of the Universe.

We are linked to each other with a wonderful relationship. People say there is no such thing as "coincidence." Needless to say, it is important to stay connected with the person who gave you the attunement. Adding to that, you should keep in touch with and take good care of the people you gave the attunement to. Do not forget to offer them the post-seminar lessons. You must train yourself so that you can always answer their questions and give advice to your seminar-takers. I also hope you would exchange information with each other when you develop new effective usages of Reiki.

Teaching is Learning

Teaching is learning; true learning of Reiki-ho starts when you become a Reiki Master.

I am truly delighted that I became a Reiki Master. After all, it is a Master who mostly benefits from the attunement and healing of Reiki. You will be given a lot of awareness in your seminars. I used to have little sensibility, but after meeting many people, I feel a variety of energies now. I can even tell what type of human consciousness gets attuned to what type of energy. I understand that the level of consciousness changes that of the energy flow of humans.

A tuning fork resonates with another that has the same natural frequency. Humans are a kind of tuning folk that resonate with the Universe. The difference is that the human consciousness changes its frequency easily and quickly, while a tuning fork does not. As human consciousness can resonate with both the positive and negative hado, Reiki Masters must keep the highest level of consciousness and stay attuned with the Universe.

癒しの
現代霊気法

Part II

Questions & Answers about Reiki-ho For a Deeper Understanding

Chapter 8

Frequently Asked Questions

Hand Healing: A Natural Healing Method Begun in Ancient Times

Question 1

Are there any official certification systems for a Usui Reiki practitioner/ teacher?

I found the terms of "authorized Master" and "official certification" in a Reiki school brochure.

1) What are the criteria to use the terms of "Usui Method," "Reiki-ho" and "Reiki Ryoho"?

2) Where can I receive an official certification?

The term "official certification" is widely used, probably because it would give the impression that it is approved by the government. But the criteria to become a Reiki Master are not established by any legal or governmental body. Also there is no standardized organization of Reiki in Japan, such as the *Kodo-kan* of judo or the Masters of Flower Arrangement and Tea Ceremony.

The Usui Reiki Ryoho Gakkai is run by the president and board members, and they employ strict criteria. But in the uniquely developed Western Reiki systems overseas, students become independent Masters after finishing a separate Master Level seminar or a combined Master Level/teacher-training seminar. They are allowed to hold their seminars and to issue certifications without any restrictions from their own teachers. However, when the Masters use the textbooks from their teachers, or become assistants to them, they might choose to stay in their teachers' groups. Or some may remain in the groups for more refinement even after becoming independent. In any case, "certified Master" and "official certification" are recognized only in the groups (or by individual Masters) in the Western systems.

Question 2

Can I expect the same quality of instruction from any teacher?

Since Reiki-ho systems have no official qualifications, it means there are a variety of Masters' quality and school curricula.

Do all the Masters/teachers provide the same quality?

This question is often asked by people who are thinking of taking a Reiki seminar. It is quite natural to want to learn from a superior Master, superior both technically and personally.

I used to answer this question as follows:

"There are no differences between Masters as long as they are able to teach theories and techniques properly and perform the right attunement. It would have been important to choose a teacher carefully if great endeavor or a lot of hard work was needed to learn Reiki-ho, like in the case of the martial arts, Qigong, sports or arts. But it requires neither great efforts nor intense trainings, as I have already mentioned."

However, I have changed my mind. Now, I must say this answer was not always right. After seeing many cases, I have found there are definite differences of energy levels and quality among Masters. Not only are there differences of energy levels, there are some Masters who even give a totally different kind of energy.

I guess it is because we now have more Masters with more varieties of levels. Actually there are some seminar-takers who are not sure about the effect of Reiki and who easily receive negative energies.

Reiki-ho is composed of two aspects: "to contact the Universal energy" and "to use the Universal energy." The former, to contact, in fact, has two steps: 1) to understand the essence of the Universal energy, and 2) to contact it. I mean people can receive the Universal energy only within the range of their understanding. They do not always receive the same worth of energy as other people do, even though their energy channels were opened in the same way.

So the exact definition of Reiki-ho is the combination of these three aspects: 1) to understand the essence of the Universal energy, 2) to contact the Universal energy that you have understood 3) to learn how to use it.

"Reiki is the energy of the Universal source and the hado of Love. Reiki healing is the practice of Love and Harmony. Reiki-ho is not just a technique to satisfy the desire. We should practice it for self-realization in our everyday life by cleansing and enhancement of spirit."

Although the wordings might differ in detail depending on the Masters offering it, as long as they understand the concept of Reiki-ho as the above and teach humbly, impure energy cannot be mixed into them.

Before you sign up for the class, it would be a good idea to attend a visitors' class to find out how people understand Reiki-ho and Reiki energy or what they are like after receiving the attunement from that Master. If it is difficult to attend the visitors' class, get brochures about the seminar as it would be helpful in deciding.

Question 3

What is the difference between Reiki and Qigong?

Reiki is the energy of the Universe but Reiki-ho is not the only system to use the Universal energy. I am taking Qigong lessons from a famous Chinese instructor. He teaches that Qigong uses the Universal energy. Then what is the difference between Reiki and Qigong?

Reiki is the Universal energy; anyone can use and benefit from it because the Great Universe never chooses anyone in particular. It is just like sunlight. The sun gives out its energy equally to all beings but not everyone benefits equally. If one believes that sunlight is bad for his health, he closes the door to refuse the sun, although the sun is still sending the energy to him. If we set up limitations with ourselves, we will receive limited benefits. If we release the limitation and open up our Kokoro, we can enjoy the unlimited benefits.

Usui Sensei developed and taught excellent Giho of how to resonate with and utilize Reiki, the Universal energy. Although it is described by only one phrase, "the Universal energy," there are wide ranges of wavelength—from the most positive to the most negative. Their levels are too many to count.

Qigong also utilizes the Universal energy, but the energy level greatly depends on the depth of the consciousness and self-discipline of the practitioner. They use the same vibrational level of energy as Reiki if they can connect to the higher vibrations. But when they cannot keep a clear consciousness they will end up connecting to negative energies. Consequently, they lose a lot of life force, send negative energies or align inharmonious energies. It is very difficult to sense and raise the level of their own energy if they do not have a lot of experience.

Qigong, in general, is a wonderful skill. But there are diverse techniques and theories in each school, as it has a long history of thousands of years. So the concepts and the levels have to be examined one by one. It is quite difficult to master Qigong perfectly. The reason for this is that the practitioners control the energy by their strong power of consciousness, which they attained by rigorous trainings. The power gained by the concentration can be easily deteriorated when they drop their guard.

Reiki-ho, on the other hand, is safe and effective because you do not need to use consciousness, as Reiki energy is not acquired by trainings. You are set up to resonate with the supreme energy by the attunement. All you have to do is just put your hands on. The energy needed for cleansing and healing effortlessly flows from your hands without concentration.

It is important to apply the hands without any intention to control something. If you try to make useless, ponderous efforts to send stronger power, other kinds of power (non-Reiki energies) could be mixed in.

Question 4

Why don't we need concentration or long-term practice?

You explained that our energy level depends on our consciousness and self-discipline. Then, isn't it necessary to practice concentrating one's mind to connect with the higher dimension of energy? Don't we need to train ourselves to enhance our concentration?

In general, it is inevitable that we make an effort and concentrate to learn something. But when we receive the benefit from the Universal energy, we need to relax and open our minds and trust the Universe. And it would be more complete if you could simply "feel" the energy instead of concentrating to feel it.

I think that we, humans, have two kinds of computers. One is a PC (personal computer) within you and the other is a terminal that connects to the host computer of the Universe. The PC has a high quality system, and it manages almost everything for you. It is contrivable to upgrade by developing more software and adding more options. You might feel confident that you could do anything with it. But suddenly, you realize its capacity is limited even though it is high-performance. You cannot keep upgrading endlessly.

Now it is time to remember the terminal that connects to the host computer of the Universe. If you can use this terminal, the capacity and power have no limitations. But you cannot just use this function even if there is a connecting device. The process to connect your PC to the terminal is "the attunement." There is no need to make any effort or use any concentration. The installation is done by the professional fitter. What you should do is 'to decide' what you do by your PC.

Of course there are some other ways to get connected to the host computer instead of an energy transmission: Usui Sensei or Mr. Hikaru Takatsuka were both suddenly given the power; or you can get it by "ascetic" training or intense concentration. You can try, if you insist. But it would probably require extraordinary efforts and many years.

The easiest way is to let the expert Reiki Master open the energy channel and just focus on its utilization. I mean, your best efforts must be dedicated to *use* the energy to increase the quality of daily life, not for the installation (opening the energy channel).

Question 5

How can we upgrade the capacity of the PC within us?

Isn't it better to use the function to connect to the host computer of the Universe rather than a PC that has limited ability?

I spoke about two kinds of computers in the previous question. I do not want you to misunderstand me in thinking that the computer of the Universe is important and the PC is useless. Both of them have, originally, the same quality—the PC, especially, is set in our brain to allow us to lead a meaningful life. And we cannot live without it as human beings, with a physical body on this earth.

We can use the PC freely but we tend to use it for personal desires because the PC in our brain is mostly controlled by our ego, which wants to be satisfied and defended. But the ego is never satisfied so our desires keep escalating and eventually surmount the PC's capacity. And while the PC equipped in our brain was originally designed to connect automatically to the Universe's computer when it exceeded the limit (and in this sense, the energy transmission would not be the only way to get connected to the Universe), unfortunately, ego (self-centered mind) cuts the connection to the host computer because the egoistic wavelength is totally different from that of the Great Universe.

As you already know, only the hado of Love (the other end of ego) smoothly accesses the computer of the Universe. Only the hado of Love resonates with that of the Universal energy. By pursuing material objects and trying to satisfy the selfish desires in this affluent society, we have left "Love" somewhere else. As a result of this, we have lost our natural-born ability to connect to the Universe's computer.

We, as human beings, first of all, should use our internal computers to actualize ourselves in full conformity with the laws of Nature. This is the best and natural way to connect to the Universal computer. But when you feel that you are struggling in this modern society, you can consider taking the energy transmission as the second best possibility. That is the significance of Reiki-ho today.

In any generation, there are always gifted people who for reasons unknown to us are given the special power to accomplish their missions. On the other hand, when you are not ready, you cannot accept it, even though it is within close reach and open to everybody. It means, as I understand it, that when the energy transmission enabled you to communicate with the Universe, you were granted the special mission from the Universe just like those gifted people.

Question 6

Do we lose Ki when we give it to others?

My Qigong teacher says "Ki is just like money, easy to spend and hard to save. If you give Ki to others too much while Gaiki healing, you would consume the life energy irrevocably." Is it the same with Reiki?

People often ask me, "Don't you get exhausted after you heal others?" Certainly, some Qigong books say, "You should not give the Gaiki treatment (the therapy to take in Ki and then give it away to the patient) too much; otherwise you can injure your health." I guess it could be true because those books introduce many examples: a well-known Chinese Qigong Master vomits blood and collapses; it is not allowed to treat more than three patients a day; and so on. Doctor Lim, a famous Qigong anesthesiologist, says in his book and seminar that it is dangerous to perform the Gaiki healing treatment because it drains so much energy from you.

But it does not mean that all Chinese Qigong experts lose energy while healing. A few of them do not get exhausted and even feel better afterwards. A great Qigong Master states that Gaiki healing is too dangerous for those who mastered only Shoshuten-ho (the technique to take Ki in and enhance one's own energy). It is just like discharging the energy you have condensed in the body and then wasting it after all so that you feel exhausted. But those who have mastered Daishuten-ho (the technique to let energy circulate between them and the Universal dimension) can practice Gaiki healing and feel even more energetic because the Universal energy just flows through their bodies.

In general, apprentices receive the same kind of Ki as their Master. And it is quite natural that they repeatedly learn from the Master's experiences and theories. If the Master teaches that he loses his own energy after giving too much to others, then the same thing happens to the apprentices. (Succeeding Ki means also succeeding consciousness and recognition.)

I think there are big differences between power that has been gifted and power that has been received through training. You have to meditate/concentrate and collect the image of the power when you get power through practices. Of course one can get quite a lot of power by concentration. When a Gaiki healer tries to send Ki to his patient by strong concentration, there is no thought that he is just a medium of the Universal energy. But, when you try too hard like this, the hado of Love will not resonate with you, and you would waste your energy.

People who have been gifted with a healing ability (instead of receiving it through training) can treat 50 to 70 people a day as time permits. If healing others is their mission from the Universe, how can they accomplish it if they get tired from just a few patients?

Reiki-ho heals the self and others with the hado of Love by connecting with the Universe, and there is no need to control anything. So receiver and giver can become very powerful without any signs of exhaustion. But Reiki Masters have sometimes asked me why their energy has been drained after a session, and they say they cannot give another treatment for a while. Reiki should be the clear Light, and they should receive the benefit by becoming its channel. But if those Masters cannot keep healing because of loss of energy, I wondered if the attunements had given them pure Reiki or perhaps this problem is caused by what they have on their minds during the healing session.

After talking with them carefully, I found that there were many cases of a lack of understanding about Reiki and that they were sending their own energy through unnecessary concentration. The cases in which I found problems with the energy itself were comparatively rare. These cases illustrate that to keep the energy as clear as possible and raise it as it should be can be difficult, even when the practitioner is given pure energy by the attunement.

Question 7

Do we receive negative energies?

I give Reiki healing with acupuncture and moxa treatment. I do feel the pain and suffer when I find negatively affected areas on my patient's body. And I suffer from the same symptom after the treatment. I think I get Jaki. Is there any solution to this problem?

"Receiving Jaki or negative energy" can come in tandem with "losing one's own energy (Please see Q6)."

I understand, in this context, Jaki means the stagnation of Ki. In its original state, Ki constantly circulates in the universe. Ki lets all the creatures exist in their natural form by flowing without stagnation. The human body is also kept healthy by the flow of Ki.

When the flow is stagnant for some reason, excessive Ki is accumulated in one spot. This becomes Jaki. Imagine a water stream dammed up and overflowing. It is not running as it was anymore. That causes flood, contamination and putrefaction. But it was not water itself that triggered these. It was caused by stagnation. (There is a possibility that lack of Ki might occur in the other places as the second effect of the stagnation.)

To eliminate Jaki (the excessive energy), you may apply the aura cleansing method to sweep Jaki off or practice Reiki healing to accelerate the flow of Ki. Jaki that you have eliminated would never be given to or harm anybody else. Jaki does not mean "evil energy." It is just partial stagnation of excessive Ki, so it will dissolve into the air.

Many people might think healing is applying hands and sending Ki to where it is lacking. But in many cases it only breaks up the stagnation of Ki. Of course Ki is supplied if it is lacking.

Oriental medicine defines "*Sha*" as eliminating excessive Ki and "Ho" as supplying Ki where it is lacking. Reiki healing automatically works between Sha and Ho to answer the need. When Jaki appears, the Light is shut out and dark energy occupies the mind and body. It causes various kinds of negative influences. Reiki healing brings back the Light, and we can regain the positive energy because positivity is our nature.

But there are some healers who claim that they receive Jaki or the patient's symptoms even though we assert that we cannot get Jaki from other people. To block Jaki, those healers are likely to build up barriers, which ends up stopping the smooth energy flow.

Reiki healing is performed within the resonance of Reiki energy; in this way, the healer is protected. In this safe energy field, the life energy of the healer and healee circulates. This promotes the purification and cleansing of each other.

When the receiver has negative energy inside, it once comes into the healer. Any pain, discomfort or displeasure you feel is reminding you that you yourself have the possibility of having the same negative energy as the receiver does. Sensitive healers become afraid that they might take in those unfavorable energies, and that they would stay forever. And this fear makes them build up barriers to block those energies in their body. This is the true picture of "getting Jaki from the receiver."

If you feel negative energy from others, please just watch your breathing. Just watch it calmly. Do not control it. And feel the energy flow. Relax. While you are observing the movement and sensation of the energy, it stays for some time and goes out of your body. It goes away smoothly.

When you cannot stand the discomfort, you may try these ways as tentative solutions, instead of building a barrier:

- Imagine that you wear gloves of Reiki light before healing
- Shake the hand(s) to drive away the uneasy sensation while exhaling
- Try Hikari no Kokyu-ho after healing (Inhale the Light from your crown into your whole body and exhale the Light out of the body and expand)

Question 8

Is Reiki-ho a way of achieving relaxation to relieve stress?

You told us in the explanation of Level I, that Reiki relaxes and heals the body and mind, and enhances self-healing power and the immune system. But I think Reiki works in a more mysterious way, doesn't it?

Reiki has a lot of mysteries. However, it is not an appropriate attitude for us to pursue an understanding of the mystic experiences. It is better to leave it as mystery. It is more important to make the most use of Reiki.

I believe that Reiki-ho is the best way to relax. We easily get nervous without any effort. But most of us in this modern society have forgotten how to relax. Therefore, we always feel stressed out. Stress is a warp/distortion in our body and mind. Once it occurs, it works destructively on us. The cause of this warp exists everywhere.

We have long known that there are three factors that cause illness: internal causes, external causes and neither one.

Internal causes are mostly emotions: happiness, anger, sadness, fear, astonishment, anxiety and so on. External causes are mainly natural environments: heat, cold, wind, humidity, dryness and so on. Causes that fall into the "neither ones" category are overdrinking, overeating, being overworked or oversexed, injury, addiction, parasites and heredity. Some other artificial external causes can be added in this modern society: electromagnetic waves, pharmaceutical and social drugs, food additives and air pollution.

These causes are "stressors" that *trigger* stress but they are *not* the stress themselves. First the stressors deform our body and mind and then stress is induced.

It is impossible to avoid the stressors in this society, but it does not mean that everyone is stressed out. You can run away from them, fight against them, force them away, and of course, you can try to get along with them. It is your choice. But what if there is no way to escape or you lose the fight? So if you have the skill to associate with (control, if possible) the stress, the chances of you becoming sick are very few.

There are about 20,000 kinds of illness on the earth. According to many experts, 90% of all diseases are somehow related to stress. Reiki helps us relax with a high vibration (tender and subtle hado). Reiki prevents stress and supports us by eliminating any existing stress.

"We are healthy" when the balance of energy is kept in a certain range. When the balance is disturbed for some reason and cannot go back to the original state (health), "we are sick." Health can be explained by the weight of a pendulum in a stationary position. When it is swinging, it is still healthy, because the pendulum is moving in a certain range. What if the pendulum stays on one side without coming back to its original circuit? We have to consider this condition as illness.

Energy balance is broken by stress. We are "stressed" when the body and mind are affected by the stressor. At that point, the health of our immune system and our self-healing power decreases. As a result, homeostasis, the state of balance in which we are healthy (when the pendulum returns to the center) is deteriorated.

Homeostasis is created by three systems: the immune system, the autonomic nervous system and the hormones. These systems keep each other balanced, but when just one of them fails, all the systems fail to work properly.

There are people who are not quite ill but not healthy. Their pendulums are moving in a disordered circuit. They may go off the track in the next minute. There are some people whose pendulums are keeping central points but swing very little. And there are some other cases that take more time to come back to the center when they swing to the right. Also there might be people, who though not ill, have pendulums that have unusual orbits due to their personalities. No matter what the case, we cannot stop the swing. The movement is necessary for life and the proof of our existence. Each thought, word and action at each moment affects the movement of the pendulum and accumulates over a lifetime.

Fortunately, we who have Reiki can maintain a natural and relaxed attitude and can correct any unbalanced energy state so that we can keep our pendulum in a symmetrical motion that leads to a happy life.

I have discussed ideas about healing the body and mind by relaxation. In a later chapter, I will talk more about how the ultimate relaxation of Reiki gives us the guidance to Satori/enlightenment.

Question 9

Can I self-educate by reading manuals?

A friend of mine took a Reiki seminar and lent me the textbook. It seems easy to understand. Can I teach myself by reading it?

Textbooks teach you how to utilize the healing ability after receiving it by the energy transmission. So once you have completed the Reiki level of that textbook (from any school), the book might be a great help. If it is edited for self-teaching, somehow it might be useful. Otherwise, without the energy transmission, you would not get anything from only reading textbooks; it would have no effect.

When you have not connected to the Universal energy, just learning technique does not make sense. Having no effect would not seem as if it could harm you, but just like we imagine that for the most part, playing a game doesn't cause harm, it sometimes can, and it can cause serious harm or injury. Because energy has a far-reaching influence on the ultra (super) consciousness beneath the subconscious mind, the misuse of energy could be dangerous.

There was a fortune-telling game that was popular among elementary school children. Though it was "only a game," it became a serious problem because some children fell into a trance and babbled strange things. I think they were too sensitive to the energy and responded to a hado of low dimension. When you play a game without the proper instructor, it can have very dangerous consequences.

Preventing harmful effects as described above is one of the reasons why the Reiki symbols (the medium used to connect with the energy) and the Kotodamas are not publicized. Neither a Reiki Master nor a seminar-taker should carelessly reveal textbook information or other knowledge that have been kept in secret for good reasons.

CHAPTER 9

Frequently Asked Questions about Reiki History

Question 1

Why didn't Reiki-ho become popular in Japan?

My Reiki teacher said, "Although Reiki was founded by a Japanese, Mikao Usui, the successors in Japan are very few. Yet, it has made unique development in America and is widely spread in the world."

I wonder why Reiki did not spread in Japan?

When I first took the seminar I was taught exactly the same thing and also wondered why. Later on I found out there was the group that had succeeded Usui Sensei's traditional Reiki Ryoho in Japan. Fortunately Usui Reiki Ryoho Gakkai, established by Usui Sensei, exists. I was lucky to be taught directly from the sixth president, Koyama Sensei. There are many excellent instructors (師範 *Shihan* and 師範格 *Shihan kaku*) in the Gakkai.

But concerning why it took so long for me to find out about the Gakkai, it is obvious that they were not promoting Reiki or themselves very aggressively. Therefore it was quite understandable that the American Reiki groups wrote in their manuals there were almost no successors in Japan.

Some other reasons I can think of as to why Reiki did not expand in Japan are:

First, Usui Sensei's principles; he did not like advertising. He strictly admonished his supporters to not advertise even if it could have contributed to the development and spread of Reiki.

Furthermore, he never taught Reiki-ho to his family (wife and children) because of his strong policy that it should not be monopolized by the Usui family.

As Usui Sensei granted Shinpi-den to five top officers of the Japanese Navy, I can safely state that he had a good connection to the navy and that Reiki-ho was quite accepted there. (Of course the member list of Usui Reiki Ryoho Gakkai shows that it also had a lot of civilian members.) I suppose the hard tasks that had to be done on a warship required them to keep themselves in good shape without a doctor or medicine. And treating themselves and others by Reiki-ho met their needs. It seemed that the vice admirals and rear admirals, who served as the captains of the warships, aggressively recommended the practice of Reiki-ho.

But, as WWII was escalating, the Gakkai temporary stopped this promotion. After losing the war, the navy was disbanded and the Gakkai lost its connection entirely. Then Koyama Sensei, a civilian, inherited the position of presidency of the Usui Reiki Ryoho Gakkai. From this period of time on, the Gakkai gradually changed its policy from one of open lecture, which was Usui Sensei's will, to one of home therapy within a members-only society.

Speaking of the navy, there are some anecdotal stories. "The Japanese navy adopted Reiki as strategy" and "the American occupation forces prohibited it because it had a strong relationship with the Japanese navy." But those stories are not supported by the facts.

Next, although Hayashi Sensei advertised to the public that he taught "Usui" Reiki Ryoho after he had become independent of the Gakkai, he actually taught "Hayashi" Reiki. He adopted his own theories and techniques aimed at curing diseases. There are still some of Hayashi Sensei's students in Japan, but they are quite old now.

One of the reasons why Usui Reiki Ryoho Gakkai had very few Shinpi-den practitioners was because they had to make great efforts to enhance their ability by themselves. Receiving the first energy transmission at Sho-den was rather easy, but it was quite difficult to keep up the patience that was required to go further.

Of course there are successors of Dento Reiki outside the Gakkai. I mean there are those who were separated or became independent from the Gakkai after learning from it. But they are few and old now. Many of them do not declare that they are "Reiki Ryoho practitioners/healers" because there used to be a period of time when hand healing was tightly regulated by the Medical Act. Many of those groups took measures to avoid misunderstandings: having other names, using Reiki energy with other treatment techniques, organizing members-only systems to exclude others, and so on.

Question 2

Why are there so many false stories about Usui Sensei?

He passed away in 1926; it is not that long ago. Why have there been so many false rumors and legends about him going around in this short period of time?

Usui Sensei left very little information about himself, although he rendered distinguished service to establish his fame as "the restorer of *Teate*

Usui Sensei

Ryoho (hand healing)." There are two reasons: he was not known in public at all until he started Usui Reiki Ryoho, and he had only four years between the time of the foundation of the Gakkai and his death.

There are false stories that he was the president of Doshisha University[22] or that he was a Christian minister. I suppose these might have been stories made-up with considerable tact rather than misinformation; with those "stories" Reiki was accepted more easily in the Christian society in America. Reiki Ryoho was inspired when Usui Sensei was fasting on Mt. Kurama. If he had been a Christian, it is unthinkable that it was Mt. Kurama, which was a sacred place for Buddhists.

There are other "stories" about how he started Reiki Ryoho; one says that Usui Sensei's long study of the Universal energy of ancient Tibet and his decoding of Sanskrit letters gave him the hint to fast which, consequently, initiated him to the energy as he had expected. But Usui Sensei wrote in 霊気療法必携 (Reiki Ryoho Hikkei[23]), *"It is difficult to explain what it exactly is. I realized that I was granted the healing ability accidentally when I felt the sacred energy and got initiated by the mysterious way while fasting."* This shows that he did not know the fundamental nature of Reiki energy because it happened to be given to him during fasting. It means he did not fast with the intention of getting the healing ability. Also he wrote, *"I was not taught this method by anyone else. I have never studied to get this intuitive power."* So the story that he studied for a long time does not apply after all.

I will not go into every detail of those false stories. What is written on 臼井先生功徳之碑 (Usui Sensei Kudoku no Hi) is almost completely correct as to his personal history. His teaching philosophy is left in the Go-kai. He also handed down the method of *Hatsurei-ho* for self-purifying and self-growth.

Last year I received valuable information from Mr. Sadao Kotani, who practices healing by Ki and Light at the Kotani Clinic in Hiroshima City: the photos of Usui Sensei, a copy of *Reiki Ryoho no Shiori* by the Usui Reiki Ryoho Gakkai (a booklet that was sold only to the Gakkai members), certificates

[22] 同志社大学 Doshisha University: a Christian University in Kyoto.

[23] 必携 Hikkei: handbook, guide, reference book, companion.

(the acknowledgement of completion of Usui Reiki Ryoho) and copies of the authorization that allowed the member to give healing to other people.

Also the research shows both the Chiba family (offspring of the Kanmu Taira family) and the Usui family (offspring of the Chiba family) have Tsukiboshi (moon and star) as their kamon (family crest).

Yet, there are still so many unclear points about Usui Sensei's life. I would be happy to cooperate with other people to find out more facts.

Question 3

How did Usui Sensei perceive Reiki?

Now that I understand that Reiki is the Universal energy, I want to know how he understood and explained Reiki.

Let us look at Usui Sensei's recognition written in 霊気療法指針[24] (Reiki Ryoho *Shishin*) and other materials.

1) *"Every thing in the Universe possesses Reiki without any exception."*

   This explains about the essence of Reiki. Modern science concludes, "Every existence in the universe consists of hado and the only difference is oscillation." These existences are corpuscle (particle) and at the same time, they are hado and energy. So Reiki is hado and energy. Moreover Reiki energy is the hado that has high and fine oscillation.

2) *Reiki Ryoho is a unique healing method based on 霊能 Reino[25] of the Universe."*

   Usui Sensei recognized that Reiki healing is done by energy from the Universal Source. I find profound meaning in his words, *"based on Reino of the Universe."* I understand that Reiki-ho is the utilization of the Reino that fills the Universe, the mysterious and precious energy of the Universe's consciousness, the energy of Love, Harmony and Healing.

3) *"Reiki Ryoho can be understood as both spiritual healing and physical treatment; Ki and Light emanate from the entire body, especially from the eyes, hands and mouth. It is effective to gaze for a few minutes, blow the breath on or stroke with the hands."*

   This explains what Reiki Ryoho is like. He means the healing is done by the radiation of Ki and Light from whole of the human body. He clearly says that Reiki heals by Ki and Light.

[24] 指針 Shishin: guideline, guidebook, philosophy.

[25] 霊能 Reino: sacred power or energy that is ethereal, exquisite, mysterious and supernatural.

4) *"This method is open to the general public for good health, moderate thought and joy of life."*

   Usui Sensei says he teaches Reiki-ho to people at large to share physical health, spiritual peace and happy life. And he asserted, *"To monopolize the secret method exclusively for economic stability of one's own family is an ignorant tradition from the last century."*

5) *"Our missions are: first, heal Kokoro; second, make the body strong and healthy. Then, while fulfilling a peaceful and joyful life, we should heal the patients around us to enhance the happiness of the self and others."*

   Usui Sensei explains how we should use Reiki. The basis of Reiki-ho is to have a wholesome spirit and body so that we can live life fully. Furthermore, he inspires us to devote ourselves to heal others with the Love of Reiki. This attitude allows us to promote the health of the self and others. He says it is our mission.

6) *"Scientists and experts have been studying the essential nature of Reiki. But it is difficult to clarify even though I am the founder. Modern science has not defined what it is yet, but the time when science explains it will surely come."*

   Usui Sensei expected that future science would find out the essence of Reiki. But still now, it is yet to be defined. I think we should leave mystery as the way it is without far-fetched arguments, and focus on how to use Reiki.

Question 4

What is the true teaching of Usui Sensei?

Reiki is "the healing of body and mind by Reiki energy." Reiki-ho at present is useful for spiritual awakening and the enhancement of consciousness. Did he teach those points? What was his true teaching?

Above and beyond all the many teachings he left, I think what Usui Sensei truly wanted to do is share his Satori with many people.

He especially emphasized this when teaching. *"The Natural Law of the Great Universe and each human spirit as a small universe, must be constantly united and exist as One."* Actually, this is the state of Satori he experienced. *"I am the Universe. The Universe is me."* He also taught, *"The Universe exists in me, and I exist in the Universe." "Komyo exists in me and I exist in Komyo."* All of these state the same thing—the unification with the Universe.

Usui Sensei used plain words to make Reiki Ryoho easy to learn for anybody. He did not mention the guidance to Satori to regular members. He taught them about healing the body and mind for the self and others, about the joy of life and the enhancement of happiness. He only emphasized health and happiness on a personal level. I think it is understandable because people in general were too poor to go see a doctor even when they were seriously sick, and most of them joined the Gakkai for the purpose of curing diseases. I suppose Usui Sensei considered this background of the general people in the Taisho period and named his method "*Shinshin*[26]*· Kaizen*[27] (Improvement of Mind and Body) Usui Reiki Ryoho Gakkai."

As I mentioned, the Gakkai's principles are: *"the maintenance of health, improvement of body and mind, and the enhancement of peace, prosperity and happiness of family, society, country and the world."* So the old Gakkai members said that Usui Sensei taught the way to Satori very intensely to those who had achieved a certain level.

Usui Sensei taught, *"The training according to the Natural Law of this whole world develops human's spirituality. When you are convinced of this Truth, your committed training actualizes the unification with the Universe. The word you speak and the action you take becomes One with the Universe and they effortlessly work as the absolute limitlessness. This is, in other words, the true nature of the human."*

On the other hand, he strongly admonished, *"Medical science is developing remarkably these days so we should not disregard modern medicine or medical treatment. That is very imprudent to do."* He taught, *"Provide Reiki healing voluntarily to the patients abandoned by medicine."* He asserted, *"There is no disease that Reiki cannot heal, so keep working hard with pure spirit."* He also taught, *"There is only one thing that Reiki and medicine cannot cure. That is the moment when the person's life is destined to end. The human is mortal regardless of age. That is the natural providence and it is inevitable. But when you know he or she is ending life, do the best and treat the person even more kindly and earnestly until the last moment. It is certain that the person will have a peaceful moment to pass away."*

[26] 心身 Shinshin: mind and body, kokoro and body.

[27] 改善 Kaizen: improvement.

Question 5

What is Go-kai?

Usui Sensei left an important teaching: Go-kai. What is the meaning of it?

Dento Reiki members recite 五戒 (Go-kai), and 御製[28] (*Gyosei*) (和歌 waka[29]) by the Meiji Emperor every morning and evening. They are food for Kokoro and the fundamental philosophy of life in Dento Reiki.

The Go-kai has two titles; 招福の秘法 "*Shofuku no Hiho*" (the secret method to invite happiness) and 萬病の霊薬 "*Manbyo no Reiyaku*" (the miraculous remedy/elixir for all diseases.) After the five short teachings it continues, 朝夕 "*Asa yu*" (Morning and night), 合掌して "*Gassho shite*" (with your hands in Gassho), 心に念じ "*Kokoro ni nenji*" (Put them in your Kokoro) and 口に唱えよ "*Kuchi ni tonaeyo*" (recite).

The Go-kai is quite short and simple but has the profound meaning of Satori, which Usui Sensei had achieved:

今日だけは "*Kyou dake wa*" (For today)
怒るな "*Ikaru na*" (Do not be angry)
心配すな "*Shinpai suna*" (Do not worry)
感謝して "*Kansha shite*" (Be thankful)
業をはげめ "*Gyou wo hageme*" (Do what you are meant to do)
人に親切に "*Hito ni shinsetsu ni*" (Be kind to others.)

Let me explain each sentence briefly:

1) 今日だけは "Kyou dake wa" (For today)
   Usui Sensei preaches the value of today in our life lesson on the earth. What actually exists is only the present; neither past nor future. Today is the whole of life. Today is an accumulation of each moment and how we live this single moment dictates our future. It teaches us that we should live for this moment, this day. "For today" modifies all the following five sentences.
2) 怒るな "Ikaru na" (Do not be angry)
   This explains that anger hurts both others and ourselves, so we should not have such a notion. I interpret that we should not be badly affected by any emotions, not only anger. The more selfish we are, the more

[28] 御製 Gyosei: waka of the emperor.

[29] 和歌 Waka/Tanka: a Japanese poem that consists of 31 syllables.

emotional we can be. The strong emotions such as anger, resentment or hatred can easily escalate and ruin our life. By utilizing Reiki we can keep our mind and spirit in harmony.

3) 心配すな "Shinpai suna" (Do not worry)
After doing what we could do today, we should trust the Universe and have a peaceful Kokoro without anxiety as a Chinese set phrase says: "Do your best and leave the rest to Providence." Anxiety and worry attract other negative energies because they have the same wavelength. Level III of Reiki-ho is the step to "believe and trust the Universe."

4) 感謝して "Kansha shite" (Be thankful)
The fact is we are not living by ourselves, but are given life from the Universe. When we truly know this Truth, we simply feel gratitude to others and the Universe. The gratitude is the energy from high consciousness that only the human has. We lose our true Kokoro when we forget the gratification and gratitude. When we are always with Reiki and receive the benefit from it, the feeling of appreciation comes over us quite naturally.

5) 業をはげめ "Gyou wo hageme" (Do what you are meant to do)
It is said that laziness is faithless to self and ill to society. We grow and learn a lot through daily life and work. People say, "What counts is not our occupation but what we learn from it." There used to be a popular belief that we must live alone, far from ordinary society for the intensive training it takes to get a peaceful mind. But we are given life with a physical body, so it is more natural to learn through routine work, everyday life and interaction with other people. Reiki-ho shows how to exercise this in the real world.

6) 人に親切に "Hito ni shinsetsu ni" (Be kind to others)
This teaches that we should recognize that others are important as well as ourselves, instead of having only selfish desires. We cannot manifest our full abilities or carry on daily living all alone. Healthy community cannot be built unless people help each other. There is no difference between self and others from the perspective of the Universe. We are the existence of the same spirit. So being kind to others means, in other words, to love yourself. You will accept and develop this idea naturally by practicing Reiki-ho; it is the lesson of Love and Harmony.

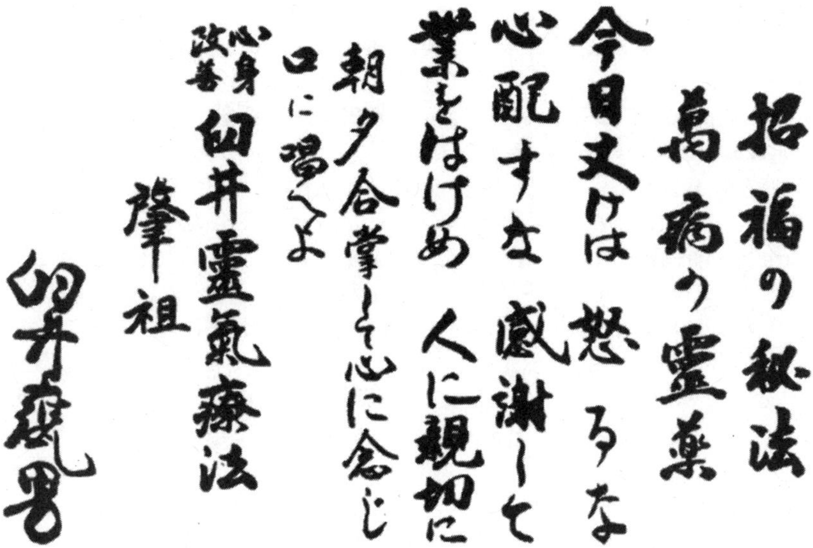
招福の秘法
萬病の霊薬
今日丈けは 怒るな
心配すな 感謝して
業をはげめ 人に親切に
朝夕合掌して心に念じ
口に唱へよ
心身改善 臼井霊氣療法
肇祖
臼井甕男

A copy of "Go-kai" given by Koyama Sensei

The Secret Method to Invite Happiness
The Miraculous Remedy for all Diseases

For today — Do not be angry
Do not worry — Be thankful
Do what you are meant to do — Be kind to others

Morning and night, with your hands in Gassho
Put them in your kokoro and recite

Improvement of Mind and Body

Usui Reiki Ryoho

Founder
Mikao Usui

Question 6

What are the names of the Shinpi-den practitioners certified by Usui sensei?

You explain that Usui sensei trained 21 Shinpi-den members. Is there any name list with all of them left?

Usui Reiki Ryoho Gakkai lost all the document and materials when its office building was burnt down and the members, who were there, lost lives by the great Tokyo Air Raid (1945) at the end of World War II. There is no way to confirm because the Gakkai has no recorded information at all.

Here I have a copy of the board member list as of July 31st, 1927. It was 16 months after Usui sensei's death. It was provided by Mr. K in Chiba Prefecture, who read my second book, 'Reiki: the Energy Fills the Universe (2005).' The source material was a 250-page booklet titled 心身改善臼井霊気療法学会入門者名簿 'Improvement of mind and body, Usui Reiki Ryoho Gakkai, name list of memberships' (14.5 cm H x 10.5 cm W).

I received 15 page-copy of it from him, which first introduces the 18 board members;

The president 牛田従三郎 Juzaburo Ushida (大師範 Dai Shihan)
Four directors 理事 (two Dai Shihans and two Shihans)
Twelve trustees 評議員 (three Dai Shihans and nine Shihans)
One account manager 幹事 (general affairs manager)

Chujiro Hayashi sensei was a Shihan as a director but not a Dai Shihan. 渡辺義治 Yoshiharu Watanabe sensei (the 4th president) or women were not board members.

Then it writes the address of the Tokyo head office and 37 branches outside, and the names of 世話役 local facilitators (care takers). It indicates some of the board members in Tokyo served concurrently as local facilitators. 江口俊博 Toshihiro Eguchi was a facilitator of 甲府 Kofu branch before he left the Gakkai to be independent that year. It says there were about 3,500 members in Usui Reiki Ryoho Gakkai.

Although it really is precious information, we can not confirm how the 2nd president, Ushida sensei's intention reflected on the list and why they did not put women on it because there is no lists when Usui sensei was alive or Ushida sensei had just been assigned as the president. I somehow grasp all the names of 21 persons from other documents but they are not finally proved as facts.

So let me merely introduce the Dai Shihans' names and some well-known Shihans in the Gakkai.

The important thing is Usui sensei's true teaching, not a list of trainees. I hope someday the 21 Shinpi-den members trained by Usui sensei will become clear like the 22 masters of Takata sensei.

Some of the Shinpi-den practitioners, as of July 31st, 1927

大師範 Dai Shihan:	牛田 従三郎	Juzaburo Ushida
	秋吉 照一	Teruichi Akiyoshi
	江口 金馬	Kinba Eguchi
	武富 咸一	Kan'ichi Taketomi
	苫米地 義三	Gizo Tomabechi
	常松 憲三	Kenzo Tsunematsu
師範 Shihan:	林 忠次郎	Chujiro Hayashi
	今泉 哲太郎	Tetsutaro Imaizumi
	江田 敬三郎	Keizaburo Eda
	藤 茂木	Shigeki Fuji
	三根 梅太郎	Umetaro Mine
	和波 豊一	Hoichi Wanami

Question 7

Why was Reiki re-introduced in Japan?

Reiki Ryoho went to America, became REIKI and uniquely developed around the world, then traveled back to Japan. Why now, and why is it spreading here?

Ms. Mieko Mitsui, a journalist and Reiki teacher of the Radiance Technique in New York, translated and published *The Reiki Factor* by Dr. Barbara Ray. It triggered the quick spread of Reiki in Japan.

Adding to Mitsui Sensei's foresight, it was the right time to accept the spiritual healing: the countdown to the twenty-first century had started, the end-of-the-world prophesy and occultism were attracting people's attention, environmental destruction and moral decadence emerged as social problems, although at the same time, people were enjoying more material wealth. Before the return of Reiki, the New Age ideas from Europe had already been introduced in Japan. It seems that enough preparation had been made for Reiki. No wonder this new healing, which was born in Japan and grew up in America, made an impressive debut here.

This sensation sent people to America to study advanced levels. And Reiki Masters from abroad have begun visiting Japan to train new practitioners and Masters, one after another. Publishing books to promote seminars is also encouraging the steady extension of Reiki.

When we take a bird's-eye view of this sweeping trend, Mitsui Sensei, who introduced Western Reiki, Reiki Masters from overseas and groups and individual Masters who are doing noticeable advertisements are all Light angels of a mutual mission.

Now it is time for each of us to think about the meaning of life and make strong efforts to enhance spirituality. If we do not, I am afraid it will be too late. I think the reason for Reiki's return is the guidance from the Universe. It could be easier for non-religious people to accept a "Light of higher dimension," "hado," "Love" and "Healing." This can be a great opportunity to share the wonderful Reiki healing and experience its benefits with as many people as possible.

It is undeniable that there were some hasty promotions. But from now on, the spirit of Dento Reiki will be rediscovered and the new Reiki style, the fusion of the Western and Eastern Reiki, will root deeply in this country.

Let me introduce one experience of mine here. On December 25, 1996, I received a telephone call from a famous Reiki teacher (who lived in Tokyo). The teacher told me that Ms. Phyllis Furumoto, a famous Reiki Master in the US, was coming to Japan informally from January 5 to 14. She was a granddaughter of Ms. Hawayo Takata and wanted to pay a courtesy visit to a person who succeeded the Usui Reiki Ryoho that had saved her grandmother's life. The teacher asked me to organize a meeting with the president of the Usui Reiki Ryoho Gakkai, Ms. Kimiko Koyama.

Koyama Sensei was 91 years old at that time. Although still active enough to walk up Mt. Kurama with the Gakkai members, she had a little hearing problem. But she understood what I told her over the phone and accepted Ms. Furumoto's request on the condition that she could go with other Gakkai members. I was going to be there with that Reiki teacher in Tokyo, but the meeting was canceled at the last moment. He told me that Ms. Furumoto's private visit was advertised to many people and she could not change the date. Later, it turned out be an 'official' reason. He confessed me that one of the teachers who came with Ms. Furumoto said to him, "Reiki-ho's originator is American, not Japanese." He canceled the meeting to prevent showing a disrespectful attitude to Koyama Sensei.

The Masters from overseas are proud that it is they who made Reiki last this long. They think their "Reiki" is not the "Reiki Ryoho" of Mikao Usui anymore. I guess their self-confidence might have allowed the teacher to say,

"Reiki-ho's originator is us."

On the other hand, one well-known Japanese teacher says that we no longer have anything to learn from abroad. I am not judging whether either statement is right or wrong. But, actually, some motivated Japanese teachers are starting to feel the limitations of Western Reiki.

I suppose many Masters (teachers) are going to stand at a crossroads, looking at the two different ways—towards the East or West or at the Gendai Reiki Healing Association, which has merged the East with the West.

Question 8

What is the difference between Dento and Western Reiki?

Could you please explain in detail about the differences between Dento Reiki, which succeeds from the tradition of Usui Sensei, and Western Reiki, which came back to Japan from America?

Dento Reiki has strictly kept the form and processes developed by Usui Sensei. Its followers try to carry on the exact Kokoro of Usui Sensei, not just the healing techniques. Its practices are full of the solemnity of the truth seeker. Western Reiki, on the other hand, is arranged in a practical and simplified way with European and American ideas.

There are usually four steps in Western Reiki—Level I to IV—while Dento Reiki has only three: Sho-den, Oku-den and Shinpi-den." The energy transmission to open the channel of Reiki flow, reiju, is the "attunement" or "initiation" of Western Reiki.

I think most of you already know about the Western Reiki method so let's look at the outline of Dento Reiki.

There are three important points for teaching:

1) To select 125 Gyosei of the Meiji Emperor as the food of Kokoro
2) To carry out Go-kai, and make efforts to raise spirituality (and personality) in daily life
3) To practice Hatsurei-ho for self-cleansing and spiritual cultivation

There are two methods to enhance internal Reiki:

1) Keep up spiritual training. The human is the small universe (microcosm) and given Great Spirit from the Great Universe (macrocosm); the more personality and spirituality a person raises, the more powerful his internal Reiki becomes.

2) Receive more reiju. This is a sequence of the formation and development method of the Reino of the Universe performed by the instructor. Attend 修養会 *Shuyo-kai*[30] as many times as possible to receive many reiju, which strengthens internal Reiki.

The program of Shuyo-kai is:

1) Clear the mind (recite Gyosei to clear the mind to be ready for reiju)
2) *Seiza*—sit down in Japanese style (close the eyes lightly in a relaxed posture)
3) Kenyoku (embody the Kokoro of *Saikai Mokuyoku*[31] to cleanse the body and mind)
4) 浄心呼吸法 *Joshin Kokyu-ho* (cleanse your Kokoro and put it into the Tanden while breathing quietly)
5) Gassho
6) *Seishin Toitsu* (center your Kokoro while in Seiza and Gassho; when you keep this posture, the Shihan gives you reiju)
7) Recite Go-kai three times (first, the Shihan leads and members repeat it after him; second, everyone recites all together; third, everyone recites and swears to practice Go-kai; fourth, pray for the health of the self and others, and for the world's peace.)

By this first reiju, they are accepted as Sho-den and allowed to perform Teate Ryoho (hand healing). Reiki will get stronger by mastering the profound aspects of the Kokoro of the Meiji Emperor's Gyosei, practicing Usui Sensei's Go-kai and attending as many Shuyo-kai as possible.

After long years of serious studying, the members develop the ability of 病腺霊感法 the Byosen Reikan-ho (the technique to sense negative energy from the source of disease as Hibiki and diagnose the symptoms and number of treatment days) and 霊示法 Reiji-ho (the technique to let hands go to affected areas automatically and start sending Reiki). And when the members reach a certain level of both of these and some other Gihos, they are accepted to Oku-den Zenki (the first half of Oku-den). And the first certificate from the Gakkai, which certifies Oku-den Koki

30 修養会 Shuyo-kai: the regular meeting of the Usui Reiki Ryoho Gakkai.

31 斎戒沐浴 Saikai Mokuyoku: the washing and purification of the body and mind before praying or before a religious ritual.

(the second half of Oku-den), is finally given to whom has developed the further ability and is qualified to complete the whole course of Usui Reiki Ryoho. No one can tell how long it might take from Sho-den to Oku-den Koki. Furthermore, Usui Sensei carefully selected spiritually advanced people among his Oku-den Koki students and enrolled them his Shinpi-den class. I understand this traditional system keeps a high level of skills and only a few members could receive Shinpi-den from Usui Sensei. Actually, it seems that those who have been studying and practicing Dento Reiki have mild and warm personalities. I suppose they all have the ability to feel the affected areas as Hibiki and let their hands be drawn (guided) effortlessly to the areas.

Compared to Dento Reiki, Western Reiki is much simpler. For example, in some Western Reiki teaching practices, students can take the Level I seminar and receive an energy transmission on Day 1 and can then attend the Level II seminar the very next day and Level III the following week without any restriction. In this curriculum they cannot be expected to have the ability to sense Hibiki or to let their hands be guided by Reiki to the affected areas. But it is systematized so that applying Reiki on the basic positions of the body will cover the problem areas.

Also, many are taught to know the standard time of applying hands on each position based on their experience: five minutes for a Level I practitioner, and two and a half minutes for Level II. This system allows any healer to heal with confidence. The sensitivity of the hands to sense the problem areas will be more developed after a while so that the practitioner will be able to heal more efficiently in time. I still remember Koyama Sensei nodding, saying "I see. That is a practical way too, isn't it?" when I told her about the basic position method.

The Western and Eastern Reiki methods have some seemingly contradictory styles. Dento Reiki features detailed training and counseling by the membership. On the other hand, Western Reiki focuses on the healer training seminar, which takes place in a short period of time, with relatively fewer schools that pay attention to extra review trainings after the seminar.

I have read a kind of "abandonment" advertisement in a magazine that says, "You do not need to take another lesson once you have received an energy transmission because Reiki is self-caring." This is not a problem if the Master teaches enough of the method to allow the student to practice after only one seminar. Reiki-ho is easy to begin with but it is important to keep raising your vibration by continual practice. While practicing, it is quite natural that some additional questions may spring up, and you will want to study again and have interactions with other practitioners.

Gendai Reiki Ho, based on the rationality of Western Reiki with the essence of Dento Reiki, is very easy to learn through its simple ideas and Giho. It is also recommended that you attend monthly Koryu-kai (gatherings) to keep practicing. We sincerely hope to contribute to the promotion and practice of Reiki-ho.

Chapter 10

Frequently Asked Questions about Reiki Techniques

Question 1

To what level of Reiki-ho should I learn?

There are four levels in Reiki-ho. I wonder which level I should learn. For me, it would be enough if I could heal my mother because she is not really healthy.

Let me tell you briefly what you learn in each level of Reiki-ho:

Level I: Acquire healing ability and learn how to cleanse energy
Level II: Increase the healing ability and learn how to heal beyond time and space
Level III: Change yourself by the guidance of the Universe
Level IV: Learn how to transmit energy, to teach and guide as a Reiki Master

What level you should learn depends on how you want to use Reiki-ho.

If you want to heal yourself, your family and pets, for now, Level I would be sufficient.

Originally, in Usui Reiki Ryoho, after receiving the first reiju of Sho-den, the students kept practicing for many years and received many reiju at Shuyo-kai to develop their ability. Upon completing this long process, they were finally allowed to take Oku-den (Level II). In this sense, Level I was never to be regarded as just the beginner's level. Even so, it would be quite natural to move on to Level II at the point when your practice of Level I encouraged you to learn more.

You might choose to learn Level II when you want to increase your healing ability because you or your family are suffering from illness, do distant healing, heal past psychological problems or use Reiki for a brighter future.

Level III allows you to use the supreme symbol and connect to your own higher consciousness. Also by continuing to receive revelation and guidance, you will become one with the hado of Reiki in your daily life, helping you to achieve spiritual advancement. You should also have had sufficient use of the symbols you learned in Level II in order to recognize their effects. At the least, you must want to raise and expand your consciousness to be spiritually awakened. I like to accept only the people with all these clear and strong reasons in my Level III seminar. In this regard, I do not want to invite you to be attuned to Level III if you just want to become "more powerful." In that case, Level II is sufficient.

Of course, I gladly accept people who understand the essence of Reiki and are seeking spiritual growth by it. I also welcome people who have great interest in Reiki-ho and want to dedicate themselves to spread it as Reiki instructors.

Question 2

How can I see a person's aura and feel energy sensation?

A friend of mine can see auras and feel energy, but I do not at all. They say the effects are the same without sensing anything in Reiki healing, but is it possible for me to develop those abilities?

Getting the energy sensing ability at an early point does give you some advantages as a healer. This does not mean these senses are an absolute necessity in order to become a healer. But if you see an aura coming out of your fingertips and feel the tingling sensations or warmth between your palms, your healing session becomes an even more enjoyable practice. It would be much better than feeling nothing. Feeling the energy circulating between you and the receiver and detecting the congested energy areas develop your healing skills as well.

You might say, "Yes, I know. But I was not born to be that sensitive. I do not feel anything at all." Of course, there are degrees of sensitivity among individuals, but it is very few who never feel anything.

The reason you cannot see an aura is, in fact, because you have never seen it before. (The same applies to feeling the energy. If you have no experience of sensing energy, you cannot feel it.) Seeing an aura is not that difficult. But for a beginner, it is almost impossible to see the subtle colors and shapes in the rainbow-like layers. There are certain factors involved that require much experience, the person's nature and an inner level of awareness to see them. However, everyone has the ability to see the part of the life force energy emanating from the fingertips.

More people say that it is easier to feel energy than see an aura, but it could be the opposite as it depends on the individual. I recommend that you try both. Once you are able to do one, then the other will be done with more ease.

Let me put it more clearly here. We have been talking about two things—seeing the aura and feeling energy. But in fact, these two are the same abilities. Every creature—human, animal, plant, mineral etc.—emanates some kind of energy. This has been recorded from antiquity in the Eastern and Western cultures. Now it is possible to film the aura using Kirlian photography. These energies are called, for example, Purana, Aura, Odo, Ki, Magnetic Life Force, Life Force Energy, Reiki, Reiko and Genki—there are many other names. These energies are a kind of Universal energy. They circulate through the Universe and work on everything that exists. (Some of them are not necessarily Reiki energy though.)

To see an aura and to feel energy, therefore, is to perceive and accept the existence of Reiki itself. Reiki practitioners can take this opportunity to feel Ki, and develop this sensitivity.

An Exercise for the Development of Sensing Ki.

Here I will explain seeing and feeling Ki, using the word "Ki" to mean energy. Although this is an exercise, please do not concentrate too hard. Just open yourself up to feel and accept what it is. Relax and wait until you see (or feel) it effortlessly.

If you have a good teacher, he or she can help you out. But it may take more time to learn the few techniques without any coaching. You are actually seeing it, but when you have no experience, you end up overlooking it. As you do not know where and how it appears, you simply fail to notice it.

This is like picking wild Matsutake mushrooms (very rare, edible mushrooms) in the bush. They are there in front of you, but you just do not recognize them. You need a guide who can show you they are there. After learning from him, you would be able to find them yourself.

How to practice on your own:

1. Gassho to connect to Reiki.
2. Rub your palms together until they become warm, visualizing that Ki is emanating from your whole body.
3. Relax your wrists and shake your hands sideways then up and down for about a minute. Put your hands about 10 centimeters apart from the Gassho position. Relax and feel Ki emanating from your palms.

I think more than 80% of the people would feel some sensation of Ki with this exercise. It might be a tingling-like, static electricity—like a spider crawling on your skin—or warmth or coolness. It depends on the person as to how he or she feels it.

When you feel these particular sensations, observe carefully the areas where they are felt. Also move your hands closer and farther apart. Try to feel the sensations and study the areas between the fingers or the space between the hands.

This next exercise is easier if done in front of a plain background such as a white wall or paper screen. Hold one hand up against the background and then try seeing Ki emanating from the fingertips and whole of your hand. At first use a dim light to avoid causing confusing shadows on the background. You should try various colors for the background because some might find certain colors to be more helpful than other colors. When you become accustomed to these sensations, you will be able to see the energy in any circumstance.

Once you understand how to see and feel it, you will soon develop the sensitivity to see Ki above people's heads and around their whole body.

If you have some difficulty about self-teaching, find a good teacher who will create the best situation for you to see Ki. This would be the easiest way rather than struggling alone.

To develop and enhance this ability to sense energy, please read Section 13 – The Self-Development System of Gendai Reiki Ho, page 137, "How to Develop Sensitivity."

Question 3

What are the Giho of Dento Reiki?

Does Dento Reiki have any special hidden, sacred teachings or methods that are different from Western Reiki? For example, magical spells, incantations or ritual hand passes?

There are no secret or mysterious Giho in Dento Reiki. Quite scientific ones are passed on, actually. Some of them have been introduced to Western Reiki, such as the Reiki Marathon (continuous healing and group healing) and the Reiki Circle (Reiki Mawashi). Generally speaking, it seems the techniques adapted into Western Reiki can be practiced by anybody. However, most of Dento Reiki Giho requires reaching a certain level of learning.

All of Dento Reiki Giho might have been taught to Hayashi Sensei and Takata Sensei. However, while they were cultivating a growing number of practitioners in America, it seems that some of the Dento Reiki techniques were left out, one after another, seemingly because they were considered to have no effects or were useless. (Actually they are effective and useful but require more skillful abilities and sensitivities.)

One such technique, for example, is Byosen Reikan-ho, which I mentioned in Question 8 of Chapter 9. This is one of the three major Gihos of Dento Reiki. Even if you are taught how to do it, you will not be able to master it until you learn to detect Hibiki, the vibrations from the source of the disease. The same applies to, for example, Reiji-ho. Again you cannot use this Giho until your hands are naturally guided to the imbalanced area.

However there are some Giho that do not require any skills or ability, such as 発霊法 Hatsurei-ho and 念達法 Nentatsu-ho. I will introduce you to these wonderful Giho in the next chapter, "Self-Purifying and Self-Growth Giho."

The following are some of Dento Reiki's main Giho;

丹田治療法 *Tanden Chiryo-ho* (detoxification technique)
へそ治療法 *Heso Chiryo-ho* (treatment on/around the navel)
血液交換法 *Ketsueki Kokan-ho* (purify the blood with Reiki)
半身交血法 *Hanshin Koketsu-ho* (upper half of the body)
全身交血法 *Zenshin Koketsu-ho* (full body)
呼気法 *Koki-ho* (blowing)
凝視法 *Gyoshi-ho* (staring)
打手治療法 *Uchi Te Chiryo-ho* (pat with hands)
撫手治療法 *Nade Te Chiryo-ho* (stroke with hands)
押手治療法 *Oshi Te Chiryo-ho* (push with the fingertips)
性癖治療法 *Seiheki Chiryo-ho* (send a message into the subconscious mind)

Question 4

What more is there to know about the Reiki symbols?
I want to know more about the Reiki symbols.
I have used the four symbols, and I feel their power. If you have any other usable symbols, please teach me.

The Reiki symbols widen the use of Reiki, and they are very versatile. I have told you that the Master Symbol is regarded as a sacred symbol to invite in something great in the Western countries. But please understand clearly that the Reiki symbols themselves are not divine or precious beings. What counts is only their function. The Reiki symbols are valuable because they provide the function of connecting to the Universe. When you enhance your consciousness to constantly be with the Universe, you are the symbol yourself and the words you speak are sacred Kotodamas. You are resonating with the Great Universe all the time. You do not need tools any more.

You must not misunderstand that the symbols themselves have some great power to rely upon. Otherwise you would worship only the images and not the reality. Try to let go of the symbols when you have developed the ability to use them properly. You have to overcome this limitation before long; it is a hurdle to clear. Please understand this concept and try not to seek more symbols or secret methods (unless you have an interest in a kind of *Mikkyo*, esoteric Buddhism).

Gendai Reiki Ho defines the Reiki symbols as "the effective tools for the beginner." The symbols have a diverse historical background, but their roles in Usui Reiki are like a floatation ring when you first learn to swim —a skilled swimmer does not need it. When you have enough resonance with Reiki, you no longer need the symbols.

Question 5

What is the final goal of Reiki-ho?

There are Levels I to IV in the Reiki system, and I do understand that each step has its unique element. After I learn all those levels, what should I aim at? What is the final goal?

Let me explain what we learn in each level from the point of view of where Reiki-ho finally goes.

In Level I, you hand-heal mostly the imbalance of the body and mind. In Level II, you learn cleansing and clearing past karma, and then creating a positive future. In Level III, you learn how to live every day filled with the Light.

After these steps the final goal is absolute Satori, enlightenment.

The term "Satori" in Gendai Reiki Ho is different from that of the religious concept. We understand it to mean achieving an absolutely relaxed state of mind and body. Disharmony and imbalance are always accompanied by some tension, strain, blockages, stiffness and stress or energy congestion. Only an absolute state of relaxation can unblock and release these conditions. This is the key to achieving a balanced state. The hindrances to relaxation are fear, sorrow and anger. These always create tension due to our self-defense mechanisms because we lack that awareness that we are given life and guided by the Universe.

To gain the state of absolute relaxation you must trust the Universe and leave everything to the Universe. Also you have to live every day in resonance with the Universe. The final goal is to reach the following states: the Universal Reiki and your internal Reiki vibrate all together harmoniously, and you are one with the Universe. It is exactly the same mind state as Usui Sensei reached.

Usui Sensei positioned the Usui Reiki Ryoho Gakkai members into ranks (等 *Tou*),[32] from the first to the sixth, according to their ability. The members who completed Sho-den, Level I, were regarded as the sixth rankers. When they reached the third rank he gave them Oku-den. The first rank remained empty, as Usui Sensei placed himself at the second rank. The reason for this empty position was that Usui Sensei expected somebody in the membership would become superior to himself. This shows his clear sentiment that he wanted members to keep up their spiritual training limitlessly. According to this faith and purpose, he taught the right attitude and the right way to live.

I would like to explain how to practice the above to people who are willing to learn. But it will be when I have another chance to tell it, as there is not enough space in this book.

[32] 等 Tou: rank, grade, degree.

癒しの
現代霊気法

Part III

Self-Purifying and Self-Growth Giho

Chapter 11

Self-Purifying Giho

霊気シャワー **Reiki Shower**

The Reiki Shower cleanses the physical body and activates the energy body by absorbing Reiki energy throughout the body like a shower.

You can practice the Reiki Shower anywhere to cleanse yourself and raise your consciousness. It is also useful to cleanse your aura. Just practicing this exercise can also bring you into a meditative state.

1. Stand or sit. Make yourself comfortable. (I will explain as if you are standing.) Close or half close your eyes. Breathe naturally, paying no attention to your breathing.
2. Gassho. Raise your arms over your head, keeping them apart. Feel that the Reiki vibration from the Universe is showering over your whole body.
3. While feeling the waves of Reiki, slide your hands, with the palms facing your body, down the surface of the front of the body, from your head to your feet over and just off the body. Reiki from your hands and the Reiki Shower from the Universe become one. Your hands are helping Reiki to wash out all the unnecessary energy through your feet. Repeat this a few more times.

   The Light of Reiki reaches to all of your cells and fills every part of your body. You will feel that Reiki is emanating especially from your eyes, hands and mouth.
4. Gassho.

Now with your whole body activated by Reiki, and your hands filled with the Light, you are ready to heal yourself and other people. When you do a Reiki Shower before and after the healing, you do not need to do aura cleansing to yourself.

光の呼吸法 **Hikari no Kokyu-ho (Light Breathing)**

This method is taken from 浄心呼吸法 *Joshin Kokyu-ho*, one of the most important procedures in Hatsurei-ho. It is simplified so that everybody can practice it anywhere and anytime. This is very effective for removing stress and tension, and cleansing the mind and body.

1. Stand or sit. Make yourself comfortable. (I will explain as if you are sitting on a chair.)
2. Close or half close your eyes. Breathe slowly and naturally at your own pace. I recommend that you breathe in and out from your nose, but you can breathe out from your mouth if it is more comfortable. Please breathe in the smoothest way for you.
3. Gassho, and calm your Kokoro.
4. Raise your arms over your head, and feel the vibration of the Light of Reiki flowing into your entire body through the arms.
5. Feeling the vibration of the Light, slowly move hands to your lap, palms up. Keep the palms relaxed and curled as if holding eggs. Put your Kokoro into the Tanden and quietly observe your breathing.
6. While breathing in, feel Reiki as the white Light coming in from your crown down to the Tanden. Reiki is spreading from the Tanden to your entire body. Feel that all of your cells are embraced by the Light of Reiki, and are being healed, one by one.

   As you breathe out, feel that the Light that is filling your entire body is permeating your skin. It becomes your aura and expands into infinite space. In this way, you gradually release stiffness and tension.

   Keep breathing like this at your own pace for a while.
7. Gassho. Shake your hands well to clear your mind.

When you first carry out Hikari no Kokyu-ho, it might be easier to close your eyes. As you keep practicing, you will find it easy to do with your eyes open, walking, standing on a commuter train or waiting for a friend in a cafe. (However, you should not try this while driving or cycling.) When you have other people around you, practice only Number 6 with your present posture (without raising hands or Gassho.) Even if you have just a little time to do this, keep practicing every day, and your mind and body will be purified more and more.

If you happen to feel negative emotions, such as anger, sorrow or fear, fill your body and mind with the Light of Reiki without hesitation.

You do not need to visualize or affirm that "My negative thought is being cleared away." Just let Reiki fill your body; it takes the negativity away. This is because darkness and light cannot exist at the same time.

合掌呼吸法 Gassho Kokyu-ho (Gassho Breathing)

Gassho Kokyu-ho is the arrangement of Seishin Toitsu-ho (concentration), which is the essential part of Hatsurei-ho. It is simplified so that everybody can practice it anywhere and anytime. When you master this technique, your mind will be full of serenity and peace without scattered thoughts or ego. You will always feel fine both mentally and physically, and be able to maintain high consciousness. It strengthens your intuition and develops the sensitivity of your hands.

1. Stand or sit. Make yourself comfortable. (I will explain as if you are standing.) Close or half close your eyes. Breathe slowly and naturally at your own pace.
2. Gassho and calm your mind.
3. Raise your arms over your head, and feel the vibration of the Light of Reiki flowing into your entire body through the arms.
4. Feeling the vibration of the Light, slowly move the hands downwards. Bring your palms together (Gassho) and hold them a little above the heart. Bring your consciousness into the Tanden and keep it still.
5. While breathing in, let Reiki come in to your body through your Gassho to fill the Tanden.
6. While breathing out, let Reiki go out of the Tanden and permeate powerfully through Gassho.
7. Keep breathing like this at your own pace for a while.
8. Gassho to finish. Shake the hands well to clear your mind.

チャクラ活性呼吸法 Chakra Kassei Kokyu-ho (Chakra Activation Breathing)

Chakra Kassei Kokyu-ho circulates Reiki throughout your entire body through breathing. It purifies your body and activates your energy. You also become meditative while exercising.

1. Stand, sit or lie down. Make yourself comfortable. (I will explain as if you are sitting on a chair.) Close or half close your eyes.
2. Gassho. Raise your arms and feel the vibration of the Light flowing into your entire body.
3. Move the hands slowly down and close your eyes. Breathe from your abdomen (breathe in as your abdomen expands and breathe out as it contracts) for a few times until you feel calm and relaxed.

4. As you breathe in, Reiki comes in through the top of your head and reaches to every cell of your being, and the Light fills your entire body. As you breathe out, feel all the tension and negative thoughts leaving your body. Repeat this breathing and then practice the Chakra Activation Breathing as follows: (the seven chakras are shown in the chart on page 129)
5. First, "the basic breathing" of the 1st, 4th and 7th chakras.
    1) Breathe in Reiki through the 1st (Root) chakra and fill the 4th (Heart) chakra with it. As you breathe out, radiate Reiki from the center of the 4th (Heart) chakra in all directions out of body.
    2) Breathe in Reiki from all directions into the 4th (Heart) chakra, and breathe out from the 7th (Crown) chakra.
    3) Breathe in from the 7th chakra to fill the 4th chakra, and then breathe out from the 4th chakra.
    4) Breathe in from the 4th chakra, breath out from the 1st chakra.

    The above procedure (#5: 1 through 4) is "the basic breathing" that activates the 1st, 4th and 7th chakras at the same time. Do "the basic breathing" three times before you move on to the next breathing.
6. Next is the breathing technique for activating each chakra. The procedure is the same as the "the basic breathing." The chakra numbers that go in the parentheses will be 4,2,3,5 and 6 respectively. That is, after "the basic breathing of 1-4-7," you breathe "1-2-7," "1-3-7," "1-5-7" and "1-6-7."
    1) Breathe in from the 1st, breathe out from the ( )th chakra then breathe in from there, and breathe out from the 7th.
    2) Breathe in from the 7th, breathe out from the ( )th chakra, then breathe in from there, breathe out from 1st.

    Move on to the next chakra.
7. Before you finish Chakra Kassei Kokyu-ho, do "the basic breathing" of the 1-4-7 chakras again. Then Gassho.

    You can fall asleep anytime during this exercise. But when you are awake and going to do something else, shake the hands to clear up your mind.
8. Practice only "the basic breathing" when you do not have much time. It is also effective enough.

Chakra	Position	Meaning	Symbolizes
7	Crown	Spirit	Enlightenment
6	Forehead (Third eye)	Vision	Super-sense
5	Throat	Communication	Pureness
4	Heart	Heart	Love
3	Upper abdomen (Solar plexus)	Power	Impression
2	Tanden	Sense	Center
1	Coccyx (Root)	Survival	Root

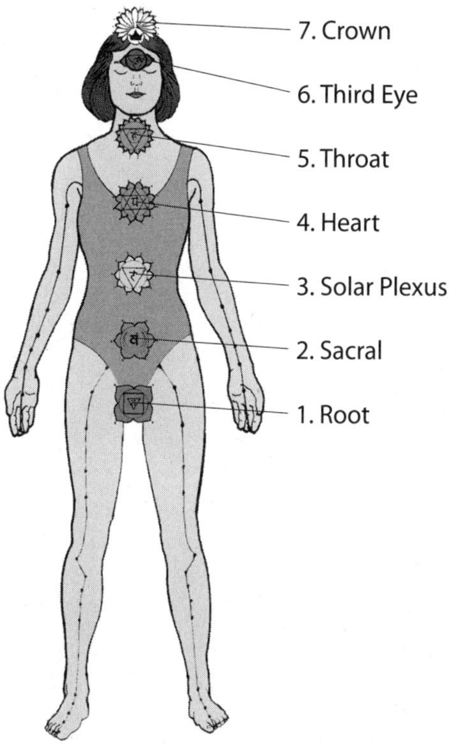

It is controversial as to where the chakras exactly are. Please practice Chakra Kassei Kokyu-ho according to this chart. The chakras are supposed to be aligned along the center line of the human body.

Chapter 12

Self-Growth Giho

細胞活性化技法 **Saibo Kassei-ka Giho (Cell Activation Technique)**

This is a healing technique to activate the cells of the entire body by lighting the imbalanced areas and sending Reiki energy there.

1. Stand or sit. Make yourself comfortable. Close your eyes lightly and straighten your back. Put your hands on your lap with the palms down when sitting.
2. Gassho. Raise your hands over the head. Feel that the positive vibration of Reiki is rushing into your entire body.
3. Feeling the vibration of the Light (Reiki), put your hands down slowly and carry out abdominal breathing through your nose. Bring your eye of Kokoro (consciousness) up to the head. Then move it downward little by little as if you are scanning the whole of your body. Try it again. If there is an imbalance, you will feel tension there. Sending Reiki energy there with the exhalation, talk to the area/cells silently as follows:

   "Thank you for giving me awareness. Now I am learning Love and Harmony by the guidance of Reiki. Please help me accomplish my learning through your role." And then move on to the next imbalanced area, and do the same thing.
4. As you master this exercise, it will become much easier; when you feel imbalance in your body, let the white Light flow to embrace it, and just say the words of gratitude: "Thank you." When you are more experienced, just a quick touch of the white Light gives enough healing.
5. You can also use your physical hand instead of the eye of Kokoro; turn your palms toward your body, and move them slowly downward over the body to sense the imbalanced area. Then talk to them as above.
6. When you have completed all the procedures, Gassho and finish with gratitude.

念達法 Nentatsu-ho (Sending Message Technique)

Nentatsu-ho is to send a message to the subconscious mind by the guidance of Reiki vibration.

1. Gassho. Raise your hands over the head. Feel that the positive vibration of the Light (Reiki) is flowing through your entire body.
2. Feeling the vibration of the Light (Reiki), move your hands down slowly. Put one hand on the forehead and the other hand on the back of your head. Bring your mind lightly to the palm on your forehead and say the following spiritual words in silence: "I am one with the Great Universe, the Great Life Force and the Great Existence." Keep your mind clear and pure while saying this.
3. 念達 Nentatsu (send message/affirm) to your subconscious mind, guided by the Reiki vibration. It could be whatever you wish to improve—for example, personality, mental attitude, lifestyle, etc.
4. After Nentatsu, move one hand from the forehead onto the other hand to cover it. Then send Reiki energy from the back of the head for a few minutes.
5. You can do this both to yourself and others. When you do this to other people, you must properly understand what they want. Nothing should be done against their will. When you practice for yourself it is more effective to do it for a short period of time many times than to do it for one long period.
6. You can also send affirmations, which are explained in the next section, to your subconscious mind by Nentatsu-ho.

The Affirmation

The English word "affirmation" could translate as "the positive declaration" in Japanese. It states that you are living a positive life. It is the commitment to your true Self.

To make your life worthwhile, first, you must have a clear vision about what you should be so that you can keep going toward it. The affirmation method helps you make it clear and actualize your true Self. It also helps you keep focusing on it so that you can send Reiki in the right direction through both the conscious and subconscious parts of your mind.

Everyone wants to have a positive, active and creative life. But if your life does not turn out as expected, instead of working harder, it might be the right time to lend your ears to your subconscious mind. "I am useless." "Nobody appreciates me." "I work hard but I do not get anywhere." "Nothing goes right." "Better to give up." If it whispers like this again and again, you are just working hard in vain. A positive affirmation can change those old messages that are recorded in your mind into new, positive and creative ones.

If you could carefully look into your true Self, you would be surprised to find the past experiences and emotions that are embedded in your subconscious mind. They are forming their own negative patterns and sending the opposite messages to your consciousness. Young children, in particular, can be easily indoctrinated with the values and viewpoints of their teachers and parents. Once those negative patterns are imprinted into the subconscious mind, it is not easy for our consciousness to accept the new and positive mental attitude.

In order to examine what kind of negative ideas are imprinted in you, you may want to talk to a counselor, or try *Naikan-ho* (a method of looking inside yourself), hypnotherapy or other treatments and therapies. They, however, require professional skills, and it is not easy to practice them without the help of a trained professional. Of course it would be a good idea to have some of these professional therapies when you have the opportunity.

But we have the affirmation method as another possibility to reach your true Self and live creatively. You can do it together with Nentatsu-ho and the Reiki Meditation.

Even if the past experiences are intensely imprinted into your subconscious mind, they cannot reach the deeper level into your spirit. It's just that the Light from your spirit is shut off. But the Light cannot be put out. It is still there. The super-consciousness, which exists deeper than your subconscious mind, knows what you should do in this life. Therefore, when you choose the right wording, you feel the vibration coming up from your true Self.

For these reasons, your affirmation must represent the voice of your spirit and not be borrowed from somebody else. But to begin with, it might be useful to employ other people's words, if they are acceptable and resonate within you. As you develop your intuition and inspiration, you will notice when something is coming out from your true Self. You can change the original affirmation to a new one anytime you find the old one does not resonate with your spirit.

The affirmation can contain both materialistic and spiritual content, because both of them are intermingled and form a perfect whole on this planet. Try some affirmations as a warm-up—nothing too serious, but representing positive intellectual interests.

After gaining some experience, it gradually becomes clear what the most suitable approach is for you.

Here is the basic way to create an affirmation: first, imagine what you want to be and become and send the image with Reiki energy into your true Self, which is deep within your heart. Lightly put your mind on your Self, and place one hand (either left or right) onto your heart and say the affirmation.

You must not try too hard or concentrate. (We often see some advertisements saying they can teach you how to gain your desires by mind power or strong visualization techniques but…) Of course your Ego can get what it wants by strong will power. But if it is not in alignment with the Law of the Universe, for example, when it disturbs your "spiritual lessons," you will end up causing another imbalance. The affirmation must be used to return to your true Self, which resonates with the vibration of the Universe. It should not be used to create any ego oriented situations.

You might find some blocks inside that impede your intention to reach your true Self. The proper affirmations melt those blocks away and bring you to a peaceful and harmonious state. The purpose of the affirmation is not to change others. You are the only one to change. If you feel that someone or something has changed around you, the fact is that YOU have made the progress necessary to recognize that change.

The affirmation must be in the present tense to assert that you have achieved it or you are on the way to achieving it, such as "I am/do" and "I am becoming/doing."

It should not express your wishes for the future—for instance, "I want to be/do." When you "wish" or "want" something in your future, you declare that you have not got it yet. It means you admit and emphasize that you are lacking it.

Doing the affirmation together with the Reiki Meditation, and letting the affirmation resonate with the Reiki symbols and Kotodamas help you receive the inspiration from the Universe.

The following are some samples of affirmations:

- I am a bright, powerful, positive and creative being.
- I am progressing day by day being embraced with the Light of Reiki.
- Reiki guides everything towards harmony and abundance.
- I really love my new job. I am in the process of achieving this job with the support of Reiki.

- I am a child of the Great Universe. It always supports me. I am a bright being filled with Love and Light.
- Everything I need in my life is already within me. I can bring out and use whatever I need whenever I need it.
- Every thing in my life happens to change it for the better. Even if it first seems to be bad, it surely turns out to be good.
- Day by day, in every way, I am getting better and better. (Emile Coue)
- From this moment I open up myself, and go into deeper knowledge, intelligence and wisdom within. (Higher-Self affirmation by Neo Reiki)
- I invoke the Light of God within. I am a clear and perfect channel. Light is my Guide. (Crystal Healing by DaEl Walker)
- I am guided by my Higher-Self, and I have the courage to change what I can change, the serenity to accept what I cannot change, and the wisdom to know the difference. This intelligence is transforming and evolving me. (Adapted from "The Serenity Prayer")

霊気瞑想法 **Reiki Meiso-ho (Reiki Meditation)**

If you already have your own meditation method, just add the Reiki symbols before you start. In this way you can fill and surround yourself with Reiki vibration. This provides you with a comfortable, peaceful and quiet surrounding where the negative vibrations cannot enter. You are perfectly protected in there.

Some Reiki schools teach that one should imagine the symbols one after another during the meditation. But you should release the symbols when you have enough experience with them. Although it is helpful to use the symbols before and after the meditation, sticking to them during the meditation is not the true nature of Reiki-ho. The essence of Reiki-ho is to resonate with Reiki and entrust everything to Reiki.

Let me introduce Reiki Meiso-ho, used with an affirmation, that you can practice every morning and night. You will realize your consciousness is rising while practicing it.

1. Stand, sit or lie down. Make yourself comfortable. (I will explain this as if you are sitting on a chair.)
2. When you are a Level III practitioner, draw the fourth symbol; if a Level II practitioner, the first symbol. Draw the symbol in the air and say the accompanying Kotodama three times silently. If you have not received the Reiki symbols yet, cleanse yourself with a Reiki Shower.

3. Raise your hands above your head, palms facing the sky, to connect with the Universe. Reiki from the Universe flows throughout your body and merges with Reiki from your hands. Your whole body is embraced by Reiki.
4. Close your eyes lightly. As you feel the vibration of Light in the palms, slowly Gassho. Straighten up your fingers. Use them as an antenna to connect to the Universe. The middle fingertips are as high as the forehead, the fifth chakra, and your thumbs are 3 –5 centimeters away over the tip of the nose. Feel you are becoming one with Reiki while breathing. If you feel any tension anywhere in your body, release it and relax. In this posture, imagine that you are breathing through your palms. (As your meditative state becomes deeper, your hands might drop down to the mouth or become wider apart and relaxed. There is no need to make your hands straighten up again. Just let it be.)
5. Slowly raise the left hand a little higher. Place your right hand on your lap, with its palm upward and the fingers curled up loosely. (If you are left-handed, do the opposite: raise the right hand and put your left hand on your lap.) You take in Reiki through the raised hand, and emanate it from the other hand. Enjoy the sensation of Reiki running through your body. (If there is any imbalance in the body, apply the dominant hand, which is on the lap, to that area.)
6. Slowly move the raised hand down onto your lap, with its palm upwards. Now both hands are on your lap. (You can make a ring with the forefinger and thumb of both hands.) In this posture feel the Love and Harmony of the Universe, and enjoy the energy interchange with the Universe.
7. Here you can place one hand (either left or right) on your heart and send Reiki energy to your Higher Self and say an affirmation. This would give you more effects. You can also put one hand on the forehead and the other on the back of the head and say an affirmation.
8. Gassho, then slowly open your eyes.

Chapter 13

The Self-Development System of Gendai Reiki Ho

Gendai Reiki Ho's Viewpoint

As I already mentioned, the final goal of Reiki-ho is Satori (enlightenment) and Gendai Reiki Ho's Satori is to gain the maximum relaxation. When you are in this relaxation, each moment of your daily life shares the same rhythm of the Universe. Gendai Reiki Ho's system of development of ability and spirituality focuses on only this point. While improving the body and mind and purifying the past karma (negative vibration) with Reiki, we are creating a bright future.

The most important factor in achieving this goal is to live this exact moment with right consciousness by the guidance of Reiki. Living life in this way is making the fullest use of Reiki.

There is not enough space in this book to introduce everything about Gendai Reiki Ho. So here, I will only expand on the explanations of the theories and processes of the three most important techniques for cleansing the mind and raising the vibration level: Hado Kokyu-ho, Hado Meio-ho and Hatsurei-ho. I also want to explain Jiko Joka Healing and how to develop energy sensitivities.

Everything is Hado

The Universe is composed of hado. "Everything that exists in the Universe is built up from hado. The only difference between each thing is frequency." This is the modern scientific conclusion as I mentioned in Chapter 1.

Most of us believe that substance exists as a real being. However, substance becomes vague when it is broken down into the molecular level, and the atomic and elementary particle levels. When it is broken down further to the quantum level, its existence becomes uncertain. This is "the uncertainty principle" of quantum mechanics. And it concludes that substance is matter (particle) and, at the same time, wave (hado).

And it is also energy. Matter transforms into a great amount of energy by a nuclear reaction, but energy can also transform back into matter. Our consciousness and thoughts are hado and energy as well.

To summarize:

1. The Universe is made of hado and all existence has the same characteristics with different frequencies.
2. Hado is energy.
3. Human consciousness is also hado and energy.
4. Human consciousness influences other things. Because all that exists is hado, human consciousness (hado) can influence other things (hado).

On the fundamental principles above, Gendai Reiki Ho aims at receiving guidance and teaching from the Universe, the most exquisite super-consciousness, by vibrating at the same frequency.

波動呼吸法 **Hado Kokyu-ho (Hado Breathing)**

Everyone knows that our mood changes our breathing. When we are mentally and physically calm, our breathing is slow and deep. When we are nervous and worried, our breathing becomes fast and shallow. When we "catch our breath," we even stop breathing for a moment. There is a witty explanation: breathing is our own Kokoro because "息" (the Japanese kanji character of breath) can be split into two parts; "自"(own, self) and "心" (Kokoro).

We can survive for a few weeks without food, a few days without water. But we would die in a few minutes without breathing. Autonomic (involuntary) nerves operate the breathing function so that we can breathe unconsciously. We can also breathe consciously, using the motor nerves (which can be voluntary or reflexive.)

The physical function of breathing is to exchange gas: taking in oxygen and letting out carbon dioxide. Adding to that, we know from our experience that breathing plays a role in switching our consciousness and connecting it to the subconscious mind. The fact that the state of mind can change breathing patterns and behavior demonstrates that both the conscious and subconscious minds are exchanging some informational signals with each other.

Why does this breathing method work? As every existence is hado, breathing itself is also hado. The frequency created by the breathing changes our own hado, and like a tuner (a synchronizing system), it attunes our hado to that of the Universe.

Superior to all breathings, Hado breathing is more effective in raising our hado with the "Haa" vibration sound to generate a precise and sacred vibration. The sound of "Haa" is the basic breathing sound, and has been since ancient times, before humans began speaking. It is said that Hado breathing is the primordial sound, which possesses spiritual power that synchronizes with the Universal energy.

Gendai Reiki Ho employs this "Haa" sound breathing as Hado Kokyu-ho (Hado Breathing Method) to develop one's abilities. You need to pay attention only to the breathing sound of "Haa." It is a simple exercise, yet very effective, and you can practice it anytime and anywhere. I would like to explain some important points here to help you practice by yourself. Please relax and enjoy.

1. Sit or stand; be comfortable. When you become skilled, you can do it standing in a crowded train. You may also practice in bed before you fall asleep or soon after you wake up. But when you are a beginner, it is advisable to do while sitting or standing to avoid falling asleep. (I will explain this as if you are sitting.)
2. Take off your socks and sit on a chair without a backrest or armrest. Place your feet on the floor, slightly apart. Put your hands on your lap, palms up. Be sure that your soles are touching the floor. Become calm and relaxed.
3. Close or half close your eyes. Release the tension from the forehead, eyes, neck and shoulders. Breathe out from the mouth with the "Haa" sound as if you are breathing a deep sigh of relief, and continue to hold the vibratory sound breath for as long as you can. At first this may last for only about 10 seconds, but it will gradually become easier. Try to hold the vibratory sound breath for 30 seconds. Be patient and keep practicing until it becomes 40 seconds. But do not try too hard.
4. Keep your mind only on the "Haa" sound as you breathe out. When you reach the limit, release the tension from the hardened abdomen. The air comes into you very naturally. You do not need to "try" abdominal or Tanden breathing; you will find yourself doing deep abdominal breathing unconsciously. There might be some other methods that include holding the breath for a moment between inhalation and exhalation, but we do not do that in Hado Kokyu-ho. Our aim in Hado Kokyu-ho is different from other breathing methods. The important point is to breathe in and out as smoothly as possible without causing

any tension. Move on from exhalation to inhalation and vice versa as smoothly as you can. Exhale evenly from beginning to end.

5. A variation of this, also good, is to open the mouth wide and try to vibrate the "Haa" sound in the oral cavity. To confirm the vibration, you can hold one hand over the ear and the other hand over the mouth. Then listen to the "Haa" sound. You can also try it in the bathtub.
6. Hado Kokyu-ho has the various health-giving physiological effects as those of abdominal breathing:
   - Improves the functions of the internal organs by moving the diaphragm up and down
   - Improves the blood flow by inhaling more oxygen
   - Improves metabolism
   - Improves the function of the autonomic nerves, the immune system and that of hormonal secretions
   - Activates and increases the energy level
   - Brings about deep relaxation and calms the mind
7. Hado Kokyu-ho also improves the function of each chakra. It generates a fine and precise vibration that synchronizes with each chakra. It activates all the chakras. It also resonates with the vibration of your consciousness and helps you create new and positive experiences.
8. You need to actually *make* the "Haa" sound until you become practiced in it. Later on, simply imagining the vibratory sound gives the same good effects.

Hado Kokyu-ho is one of the most fundamental Giho to develop and purify yourself with.

波動瞑想法 Hado Meiso-ho (Hado Meditation)

Hado Kokyu-ho, described above, invites you to a meditative state. By adding Hado Meiso-ho (the meditation with Hado Kokyu-ho), you can experience the powerful movement of the life energy.

Other meditation trainings, for example, Zen meditation or Seiza Ho, have their own particular forms and rules. The sitting styles, postures and how to move and breathe are strictly decided and not allowed to be changed. That is because these meditations could be quite dangerous if not practiced properly. While in meditation, we connect deeply with the inside of the subconscious mind and activate the life force in order to raise and cleanse our spirit. The powerful life energy deep within the subconscious mind can become dangerously out of control. There is a possibility that a mental breakdown could occur if the person's vibration is influenced by negative vibrations during the meditation. Strict forms of meditation are adhered to in order to prevent this undesirable possibility.

On the other hand, Hado Meiso-ho is based on the Hado Kokyu-ho, which has a magnificent power. As long as you follow the correct method of Hado Kokyu-ho, you are absolutely safe. The only point you should keep in mind is "to carry out Hado Kokyu-ho with the Reiki vibration in your palms." The fine and precise vibration changes our consciousness and leads us into a deeply meditative state. So, what, then, is "the meditative state"? In the meditative state, you are in tune with the super-consciousness, and you can heal yourself and still restore your true Self. The subconscious mind exists deeply below consciousness. The super-consciousness exists at a much deeper level than the subconscious mind. The super-consciousness is a higher dimensional consciousness and connects to the Universal Intelligence. Therefore, a meditative state is not only a change but also an expansion of consciousness.

1. Sit or stand; be comfortable. Straighten your back slightly so that you can carry out the deep breathing energy of hado. (I will explain the sitting position here.)
2. Sit on a chair without a backrest or armrest with your feet slightly apart. Remove your shoes and make sure that the soles of the feet are touching the floor. Put your palms on the lap facing upwards. Become calm and relaxed.
3. Close or half-close your eyes. Gassho.

   Raise your hands, open, over your head, and feel the positive hado of Reiki flow into the whole of your body through your arms.
4. Feeling the hado of the Light, lower your elbows outward to the sides of the shoulders. Bend your elbows until both hands are in front of your chest with palms down. Now your palms are parallel to the floor and the fingertips of both hands are (almost) touching each other.
5. With the Hado Kokyu-ho of "Haa" sound, push down your internal energy out of your body with the movement of your palms. (When you are seated, move your hands down along the sides of your body to prevent your hands from hitting your knees.) Feel that the internal energy is going down and leaving the body, being facilitated by your hands. Do this just once in the beginning of the meditation.

6. Move your hands upwards to just above the forehead, while breathing in. Remove any tension from the hands and shoulders. Slowly move the hands downward as if following the edge of your aura while breathing out. When you have breathed out to the limit, just relax your abdomen to let the air come into you smoothly. While you are breathing in raise the hands again then bring them down with Hado Kokyu-ho. Do this three times. Then, return to your natural breathing and keep still, feeling the movement of the energy inside your body for a while.
7. Bring up your hands and bring them down with Hado Kokyu-ho three more times. Then rest for a while. This is one set. Repeat as many sets as you want. Your body might move by the activated energy. When it moves, do not try to stop it. Allow your body to react naturally and experience the wonderful life force energy. (Just enjoy how it moves.) As you experience these sensations, you should have your eyes half closed. After a while, stop the movement with your will. If it does not stop, shake your hands in all directions and tell yourself, "I have finished the meditation." Then open your eyes. You can stop any movement this way.
8. If you see any visions or colors, just enjoy. And continue the meditation with a calm attitude. You should not get too excited or fascinated by them.

   When you become practiced, only one set of Hado meditation brings you into a state of deep meditation. As long as you carry out Hado Kokyu-ho, you can control your mind and there is no danger. (Hado Kokyu-ho protects you from the dangers of your mind floating away.)
9. Do not stop breathing intentionally. However, you might sometimes find that you have not been breathing for quite a long time. This indicates that you have entered a very deep meditation, and have moved on to a higher state.
10. When you finish the Hado meditation, shake your hands in all directions and clear your mind really well. Gassho to balance your energy before you do something else soon after this meditation.

現代霊気式発霊法 Gendai Reiki Shiki[33] Hatsurei-ho (The Gendai Reiki Style of Hatsurei-ho)

Hatsurei-ho is one of the exercises taught by Usui Sensei with the aim of spiritual growth. Spokespeople for the more recent Reiki schools are inclined

[33] 式 Shiki: style, form, method, way.

to extoll the easiness and simplicity of Reiki practice by stating that you can do healing sessions soon after the attunement and do not need further training or effort. The fact that Usui Sensei strictly taught the necessity of self-discipline and constant personal practice might surprise those schools. He strongly recommended Hatsurei-ho for spiritual advancement.

In Gendai Reiki Ho, Hatsurei-ho is arranged to fit into the practice of today's students and practitioners yet still keep Usui Sensei's ideas and teachings. I here introduce the way to practice with Hado Kokyu-ho (Hado Breathing) so that there will be no danger associated when the readers do it alone.

1. 基本姿勢 Kihon-shisei (Basic position)

   Seiza (formal Japanese sitting-position) (sit up straight on your knees with your legs bent under you) or *Agura* (sitting cross-legged on the floor). You can also sit on a chair or stand. Here I will explain as if you are sitting on the floor in Seiza position.

   Close your eyes lightly. Sit up straight with your palms facing down on your lap. Focus on the Tanden and be relaxed.
2. 黙念 *Mokunen* (Silent Prayer) Silently tell your subconscious mind, "I am starting Hatsurei-ho."
3. 乾浴 Kenyoku (Dry Bathing) This explains the Kokoro of Saikai Mokuyoku. Here you do Kenyoku with Hado Kokyu-ho.
   1) Place your right hand on the left shoulder and slide the hand down diagonally towards your right hip with Hado Kokyu, the "Haa" sound.

      (You can do Kenyoku with your hands a little above the body to cleanse your aura.)
   2) Place your left hand on the right shoulder and slide the hand down diagonally towards your left hip with Hado Kokyu.
   3) Repeat 1) again with your right hand.
   4) Place your right hand on the left shoulder. Slide the hand down the left arm to the fingertips with Hado Kokyu.
   5) Place your left hand on the right shoulder. Slide the left hand down the right arm to the fingertips with Hado Kokyu.
   6) Repeat 4) again with the right hand.
   7) Bring both hands back on your lap.
4. Connect with Reiki.

   Raise your arms over your head to connect with Reiki. The hado of Reiki will start flowing into your entire body through your arms.

5. 浄心呼吸 Joshin Kokyu (Spiritual Cleansing Breathing)
   1) Place both hands on the lap, with palms facing up and slightly curled as if holding eggs. Calmly breathe through your nose with clear and pure Kokoro. Your Kokoro is calm in the Tanden. Breathe naturally in a relaxed manner and release the tension out of your body.
   2) Inhale the white Light of Reiki from the top of your head into the Tanden. The Light filling your Tanden starts spreading throughout the body, dissolving all the tension and relaxing the entire body.
   3) As you exhale slowly and quietly with a long Hado Kokyu, "Haa" sound, the Light filling all of your body permeates the skin and expands into infinity.
6. 合掌 Gassho. Bring your palms together and hold them in front of the chest (a little above your heart).
7. 精神統一 *Seishin Touitsu* (Concentration)

   Focus on the Tanden, and imagine you are breathing through your Gassho hands, while keeping the concentration.
   1) As you inhale, draw the white Light (Reiki) in through Gassho hands and fill the Tanden with Reiki.
   2) Exhale slowly and quietly with a long Hado Kokyu, "Haa" sound. The white Light (Reiki) vigorously emanates from the Tanden out through the Gassho hands. (Keep your mind on breathing through Gassho.)
8. 黙念 Mokunen (Silent prayer)

Return your hands to your lap and tell your subconscious mind, "I am ending Hatsurei-ho."

Open your eyes. Shake your hands to clear the mind.

自己浄化ヒーリング **Jiko Joka Healing (Self-Purifying Healing)**

This method is a practice for cleansing and healing yourself and for your spiritual growth. When you have energy stagnation, Jiko Joka healing releases it out of your body. It also fills up energy stores quickly if you are lacking. In this way, you can maintain a well-balanced energy body.

1. The basic position is standing. Stand with your legs shoulder-width apart. Imagine a straight line runs through the heavens and the earth. Place the top of the head, spine and coccyx on this line. Close or half close the eyes.

2. Gassho. Raise your arms open over your head, and feel the positive vibration of Reiki flow into your entire body passing through your arms.
3. Lower your forearms as you feel the vibration of Light, with elbows facing outward. Bend your elbows until the palms are in front of the chest facing down and parallel to the ground. Your fingertips of both hands are almost touching each other.
4. While you exhale with Hado Kokyu, saying the "Haa" sound, push your internal energy down with your hands towards the ground. With the movement of your hands, the internal energy is moving down, and then flowing out from the bottom of your feet. Do this just once at the beginning of Jiko Joka Healing.
5. When you have completely exhaled, inhale gently through your nose as you raise your arms slowly with your palms still facing down. Slowly pull the energy from the Earth upward through the body in the direction of the heavens.

   Your hands are high over the head with the palms facing up. Release the energy from the Earth to the heavens. At the same time, take in the energy from the heavens and turn your palms toward your head.

   As you exhale with Hado Kokyu and lower your palms to face your body, move the hands down to conduct the energy towards the Earth. Facilitate the energy down through your head, face, chest and stomach and let it flow through the bottom of your feet.
6. When you have completely exhaled, gently inhale from the nose as you raise your arms with palms down, and conduct the energy from the Earth upward and release it above your head. Then, take in the energy from the heavens, turn your palms toward yourself and lead the energy toward the ground with Hado Kokyu. Your palms are facing downward when rising and toward your body when pushing down.

Jiko Joka Healing is a very comfortable and effective healing technique to purify and activate the energy. Please practice it as often as you want, and whenever and wherever possible.

How to Develop Sensitivity

When you pursue a career as a healer, you need to develop energy sensitivity. Of course, it could be a little bit too much to see or hear something you do not want to. But if you do not feel anything at all, you cannot have confidence about it.

In this section, let me introduce the technique for developing your sensitivity using Hado Kokyu. Select a simple but suitable method for yourself, and repeat it often instead of trying too many times at once. This approach is far more effective.

Step 1.

1. Choose the most comfortable posture for yourself. Bring the hands to chest height; rub the palms well until they become warm. Then rub the back of the hands as well. Again, rub your palms 10 times. Next, put your mind on your thumbs while rubbing your palms 10 times. Then do the same to the forefingers, middles fingers, third fingers and little fingers. Next, rub the palms again 10 times.
2. Move the hands apart. Shake the wrists up and down 20 times, and left to right 20 times. Face the palms to each other 20 centimeters apart at chest height, and feel the tingling sensations. Feel the energy emanating from the hands as you breathe out with the 'Haa' sound. Then look at the space between your hands and continue Hado Kokyu for a while. Breathe in and out from the hands.
3. Clench the hands tightly into fists and open. Do this 2 or 3 times.

Step 2.

You can do Step 2 soon after finishing Step 1. If you take some time after Step 1, you should do the rubbing and shaking hands of Step 1 before you start Step 2. (The same thing goes for Step 3. But Step 1 is not necessary if you already feel the sensation when your palms are facing each other.)

1. At the chest height, hold the hands about 20 centimeters apart, then visualize or imagine that you are holding a balloon.

   Close or half close your eyes and look at the balloon. Breathe out with the "Haa" sound; feel that the energy is going into the balloon from your palms. Your hands become wider apart as the balloon becomes larger. As you breathe in, the balloon gradually shrinks so your hands become closer to each other.
2. Continue the above for a while. When your energy perception becomes real, then breathe naturally. Feeling the tingles on the palms, move your hands closer and apart, or swirl them, to make the sensation stronger.
3. Clench and open your fists a few times.

Step 3.

1. Hold your palms over the Tanden. Keep them 10 centimeters above the Tanden. Feel the exchange of energy.
2. Move the hands to the upper abdomen area, to the chest, back of the neck, between the eyebrows and top of the head. In this way, you can develop your sensitivity. When you become skillful, you will feel the energy clearly by placing your hands over the clothes.
3. If the sensation becomes weaker during Step 3, go back to the exercise of rubbing and shaking hands and try it with Hado Kokyu. You will soon feel the energy back again.

References

Iyashi no Te, Toshitaka Mochizuki, published by Tama Shuppan.

Reiki Ryoho Hikkei, edited by Usui Reiki Ryoho Gakkai.

Reiki Ryoho no Shiori, edited by Usui Reiki Ryoho Gakkai.

FILAS, July, 1993, published by FILAS Projects.

Cho Kokyu-ho and *Cho Meiso-ho*, Suguru Tsuda, published by Goma Shobu.

Afterword

FIFTEEN YEARS HAVE PASSED since the first edition of *Iyashi no Gendai Reiki Ho*. At that time, Mikao Usui, the founder of Usui Reiki Ryoho, was commonly called "Dr. Usui." Now he is 臼井先生: "Usui Sensei," and most of the "beautiful legends" handed down with the older understandings of Reiki's history are also being updated to reflect the true story of Usui Reiki's founder and its beginnings.

In this revised edition, I have tried as much as possible to share the revelations that have emerged over the last 15 years, including information that, up until recently, had not been considered appropriate to disclose. However, I still have not been able to secure the detailed information on Usui Sensei's personal history or all the exact names of his Shinpi-den students. This is because toward the end of World War II, the main office building of the Usui Reiki Ryoho Gakkai was destroyed in the Great Tokyo Air Raids. As a result of these raids, all the people in the office at the time of the bombings were killed, and the dictated records of Usui Sensei's words along with almost all the informative documents of the Gakkai were destroyed.

There were some documents that did escape the conflagration. A picture that is believed to have been taken in January 1926 was found. This date, if correct, would mean that it was taken about two months before Usui Sensei passed away. The inscription on it says 霊授者一同 (Reiju-sha Ichido): people who were allowed to give reiju to the members, but it does not say that they all had the 神秘伝者一同 (Shinpi-den-sha Ichido) Shinpi-den title. Also found was a list of board members as of July 1927, 16 months after Usui Sensei's death. But even putting together all the information available from these two documents is not enough to identify all the Shinpi-den students of Usui Sensei. While the board members of the head office and Shihan were all Shinpi-den, we know that most of the branch chiefs in local cities were 奥伝後期 (Oku-den Koki): the second half of Oku-den and that those chiefs were also allowed to give reiju. Furthermore, we have not confirmed if there were personnel changes or not in the 16 months between Usui Sensei's death and this list's publication.

A fact that is also now known that may surprise you, Readers, is that the Gakkai has neither the 4th symbol nor mantras that correspond to each symbol. Also, after Usui Sensei passed away, Oku-den Koki became the highest grade in Dento Reiki—Shinpi-den has become merely a formality.

Usui Sensei selected those who were spiritually advanced among the Oku- den Koki students and enrolled them in the Shinpi-den class. This was his profound concern as he knew his time on Earth was coming to an end. What motivated him to start Usui Reiki Ryoho was to lead as many people as possible to the purpose of life, Anshin Ritsumei through the practice of an easy-to-learn hand healing method. He would not have been satisfied just to support a small group of elites. His true intention of the one-on-one Shinpi-den class was to mentor Shinpi-den practitioners into Anshin Ritsumei and to establish a system by which all the Gakkai members could go together to health and happiness and to cultivate human development among all those who could practice the system effectively. To actualize his intention, Shinpi-den title holders took the responsibility as board members to run the Gakkai and as Shihans to teach the members. They contributed to completing the system of the resonance with Reiki. The basics of this system were Usui Sensei's instructive messages, Go-kai, Hatsurei-ho and the Gyosei of Emperor Meiji.

After his death, there were no more lessons taught to specially selected Oku-den Koki students for the purpose of their spiritual growth, yet the Shinpi-den title has remained in use for a different purpose. When a position of Shihan or board member becomes vacant, someone from the Oku-den Koki is selected to fill the post. At the time of the inauguration of a new Shihan or board member, he or she is automatically given the Shinpi-den title. In light of this information, it is clear that today, it would be misleading to expect something more advanced in the understanding of spiritual knowledge from one with the Shinpi-den title than from any other Oku-den Koki student member of the Gakkai.

I am an Oku-den Koki practitioner, but I will not make myself available to be assigned to a Shihan or board member position even with a position vacancy. If I accepted the Shinpi-den title, my Reiki activity would be limited to practice only within the Gakkai; I could not teach Gendai Reiki Ho. Though it is simply an honorarium, holders of the title Shinpi-den instruct the members as Shihan. An Oku-den Koki practitioner is not allowed to do this. However, since I am an Oku-den member of the Gakkai, I can talk about the Gakkai in my book.

I believe that this is the first time I have written about the above facts. One thing I want you to understand is that I am the founder and a Master of Gendai Reiki Ho, not Dento Reiki, which I do not teach. The truth of Usui

Sensei and the history and Giho (techniques) of Dento Reiki were distorted abroad before. This book is intended to clarify the facts, which are verified by the documents I gathered and confirmed by the Gakkai's Shihans. And then, this book introduces Gendai Reiki Ho, which I constructed in order to share "the way to health and happiness," based on Usui Sensei's faith and purpose, to as many people as possible.

I still reverently remember Koyama Sensei's words when we last met: "Photos and documents are important of course, but what truly matters is to practice Reiki following Usui Sensei's philosophy and to become happy."

For this revised edition, Fumi Koji, a Gendai Reiki Master, made a full review of the previous translation and checked on the details with me. And William Lee Rand and his publishing company worked closely with me to insure that the concepts in this book are clearly expressed in English. I would like to express my genuine appreciation for their support and cooperation.

土居裕 Hiroshi Doi
October 2013

Hiroshi Doi Certificate for Shinshin Kaizen Usui Reiki Ryoho Gakkai

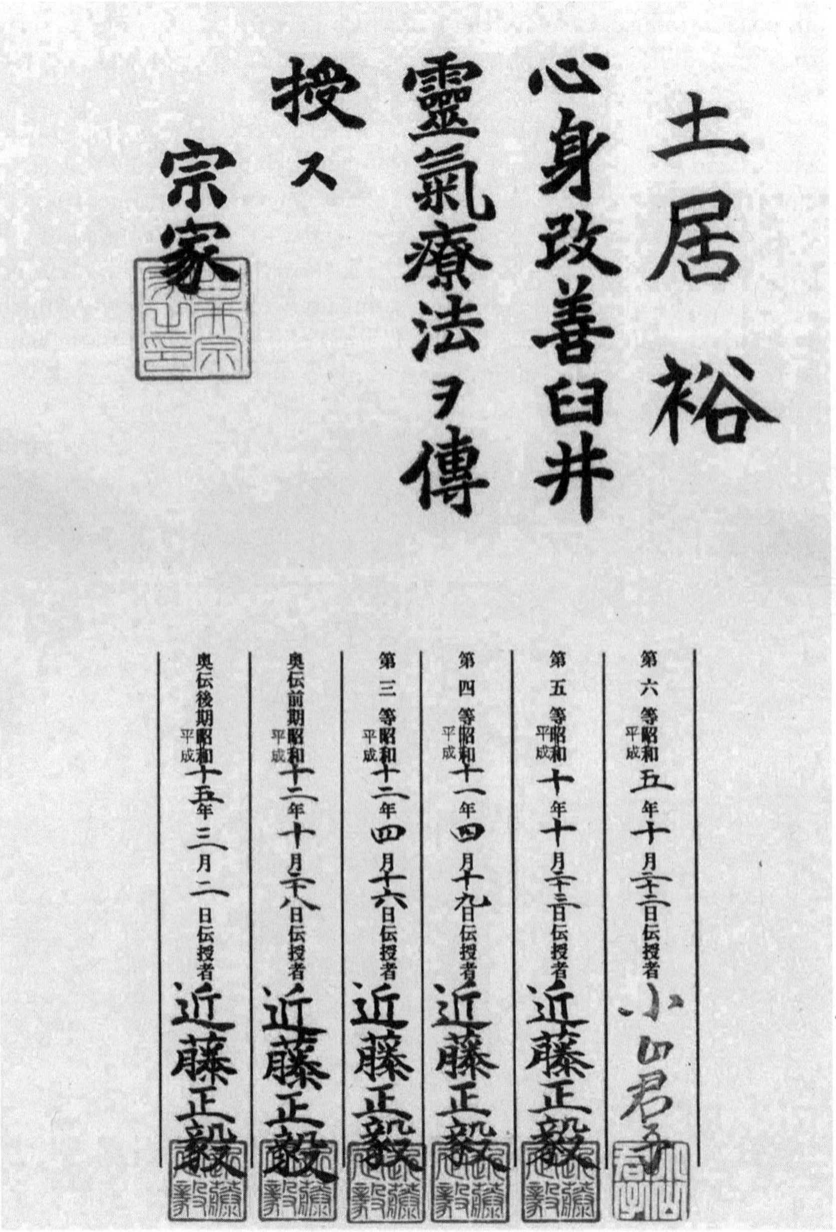

土居 裕

心身改善臼井靈氣療法ヲ傳授ス

宗家

第六等 昭和 平成 五年十月二十二日 伝授者 小山君子

第五等 昭和 平成 十年十月二十三日 伝授者 近藤正毅

第四等 昭和 平成 十一年四月十九日 伝授者 近藤正毅

第三等 昭和 平成 十二年四月十六日 伝授者 近藤正毅

奥伝前期 昭和 平成 十二年十月二十八日 伝授者 近藤正毅

奥伝後期 昭和 平成 十五年三月二日 伝授者 近藤正毅

Translation

土居 Doi (family name) 裕 Hiroshi (first name)

心身改善臼井靈氣療法ヲ傳授ス　　宗家

心身　Shin-shin; mind and body, kokoro and body
改善　Kai-zen; improvement
臼井　Usu-i
靈氣　Rei-ki These two kanji characters are written in old writing style of 霊気.
療法　Ryo-ho; healing art, therapy
傳授　Den-ju; transmit, instruct, initiate, teach, impart
傳 is the old style of writing of 伝.

The above means Hiroshi Doi was given the whole course of 'Shin-shin kai-zen Usui Reiki Ryoho'

宗家 Sou-ke, in generally term, means the founder. In the Gakkai, it meant Usui sensei. But after his death, successive 会長 Kai-cho (presidents) have inherited the authority of Usui sensei and been given this title, Sou-ke.

In Japan, stamp is sealed on certification and official documentation, instead of signing, in order to prove that it was written or approved by the exact person. This red stamp reads 臼井宗家之印 Usu-i-sou-ke-no-in, which means 'the stamp of the founder of Usui.' This stamp was used by Usui sensei, and also have been used by the successive presidents to show that they are true heirs of Usui sensei. The kanji characters of the stamp are carved according to the old and unique style of design which is quite different from the ones used in recent years.

第六等 Dai roku tou means the 6th tou. Tou is rank, level or degree. When a person is initiated the first 霊授 rei-ju, he or she becomes Dai roku tou.

The kanji characters of 昭和[34] Shou-wa were already printed on this paper before this was issued in 平成[35] Hei-sei. They crossed the name of old era, 昭和 Shou-wa, and stamped 平成 Hei-sei.

---

[34] 昭和 Shouwa (1926-1989)

[35] 平成 Heisei (1989-)

平成五年　十月　二十二日 The 5th year of Hei-sei, 1993, October 22nd
伝授者 The person who certified.
小山 Koyama (family name) 君子 Kimiko (first name).

第五等 The 5th tou
平成十年　十月　二十三日 The 10th year of Hei-sei, 1998, October 23rd
近藤 Kondo (family name) 正毅 Masaki (first name)

第四等 The 4th tou
平成十一年　四月　十九日 The 11th year of Hei-sei, 1999, April 19th

第三等 The 3rd tou
平成十二年　四月　十六日 The 12th year of Hei-sei, 2000, April 16th

奥伝　前期 Oku-den Zen-ki, the first half of Oku-den
平成十二年　十月　二十八日 The 12th year of Hei-sei, 2000, October 28th

奥伝　後期 Oku-den Ko-ki, the latter half of Oku-den
平成十五年　三月　二日 The 15th year of Hei-sei, 2003, March 2nd

The Gendai Reiki Healing Association

The Gendai Reiki Healing Association, represented by the author, offers the following activities for the sound promotion of Reiki-ho—the way to health and happiness:

1) The Gendai Reiki Koryu-kai in Ashiya City held every third Sunday afternoon is open to anyone.
2) The Gendai Reiki Ho seminar.
    a. The Basic course: Level I to IV for new and follow-up learners.
    b. The Review and Continuation course: for the practitioners who learned at other Reiki schools (regardless of the lineages); consists of review lessons of the level(s) they have already finished, followed by lessons in the higher level.
    c. Review course only: for the practitioners who learned at other Reiki schools (regardless of the lineages); review lessons of the level(s) they have already finished; no certificate issued.
    d. Master special course: for the Masters who learned at other schools (regardless of the lineages); course covers all the contents of Gendai Reiki Ho necessary to be qualified as a Gendai Reiki Master of the Gendai Reiki Healing Association.
3) The Gendai Reiki Healing Association supports the activities of the Nonprofit Organization of Gendai Reiki Network.
4) The Gendai Reiki Healing Association writes and lectures about the facts of Usui Reiki Ryoho and its founder's Kokoro.

President of Gendai Reiki Healing Association: Hiroshi Doi
E-mail: gendai-reiki@nifty.com
Website: http://www.gendaireiki.net

The NPO Gendai Reiki Network (GRN)

The Gendai Reiki Network was authorized by the Cabinet Office as a Nonprofit Organization in April 2005 for the purpose of the correct promotion of Reiki-ho. GRN was organized in response to requests from many enthusiastic Reiki practitioners.

The Gendai Reiki Network oversees the following projects aimed at making a contribution to a harmonious society where people can lead happy and healthy lives:

1) The correct promotion of Reiki (To provide ordinary citizens with the opportunity to know Reiki—the place of healing and learning)
2) The advancement of the level of Gendai Reiki Masters (To encourage them to learn more and cooperate in its promotion)

Main activities:

1) To organize Reiki Koryu-kai (gathering)
2) To organize the experience of Reiki healing for the general public
3) To organize Kensan-kai (study meeting) for Gendai Reiki Masters, New Year Reiju-kai, etc.
4) To produce and publish books, CDs and DVDs

E-mail: grn@gendaireiki.or.jp
Website: http://www.gendaireiki.or.jp/

Reiki Glossary

Anshin Ritsumei 安心立命
A state of mind in which one is always at peace regardless of what is happening in the outer world (Anshin) and while in this state to accomplish one's mission and role (Ritsumei). Usui Sensei taught that this is the purpose of life.

Byosen 病腺
The negative energy generated by the source of disease.

Byosen Reikan-ho 病腺霊感法
The Dento Reiki's healing technique to sense Hibiki by palm(s) and then send Reiki (through the palm).

Dai Anshin 大安心
The mind state that is always filled with peace, serenity and joy.

Dai Shihan 大師範
This title was created when Ushida Sensei was the president; it indicated that the Shihan was more advanced than the other Shihan. The Gakkai do not have this title now.

Dento Reiki 伝統霊気
The traditional Reiki system which the Usui Reiki Ryoho Gakkai inherited from Usui Sensei and continues to preserve and practice.

Free line フリー・ライン
Reiki systems derived from Usui Sensei and redesigned by Reiki practitioners in the West according to the practitioners' ethnicities, backgrounds and ideas.

Gaiki healing 外気ヒーリング, (External qigong) 外気功
One of the Chinese qigong therapies. The healer takes in qi (energy) by breathing or image and lets it circulate inside the body to enhance the power and quality of the qi. Gaiki healing gives the energy to the patients while the Naiki healing (internal qigong) practitioner uses it for his own health.

Gassho 合掌
To put palms together in front of the body. We do gassho when we pray and Nentatsu is done to express respect, gratitude and harmonious thought.

Gendai Reiki-shiki Hatsurei-ho 現代霊気式発霊法
Shiki means style. So this means the Gendai Reiki style of Hatsurei-ho, which is arranged for simpler and easier practice by modern people and retains the procedures and effects of traditional Hatsurei-ho of Usui Sensei.

Giho 技法
The methods, techniques, exercises and trainings to purify inner Reiki and heighten the resonance with Reiki.

Go-kai 五戒
The precept of Usui Sensei that indicates the essence of Usui Reiki Ryoho; the pathway to health and happiness. It teaches to accomplish our mission, while maintaining emotional balance and serene Kokoro and practicing love and gratitude.

Gyosei 御製
The Meiji Emperor's artistic works such as his literature, drawings, paintings and waka (poetry of 31 syllables). Usui Sensei selected 125 Gyosei out of Emperor Meiji's great number of waka poems for Reiki practitioners' spiritual advancement.

Gyoshi-ho 凝視法
Healing technique by leveling eyes, looking at and moving a line of sight onto the affected areas and sending Reiki from the eyes

Hado 波動
Wave, vibration, energy wave.

Hado Kokyu-ho (Hado Breathing) 波動呼吸法
Gendai Reiki Ho's Giho to breathe out with vibratory sound of "Haa", which is effective to let the inner Reiki resonate with the Universal Reiki. We practice this breathing during Hado Meiso-ho (Hado Meditation), Jiko Joka Healing (Self-Purifying Healing) and many other Gihos.

Hatsurei-ho 発霊法
The training Giho to enhance the quality of inner Reiki. Given to us by Usui Sensei.

Healing reaction healing crisis 好転反応
The reaction after Reiki healings and attunements caused by the rapid activation of the self-healing ability to restore the normal health condition. It creates temporary and superficial worsening of symptoms because of the release of toxins.

Heso Chiryo-ho へそ治療法
Dento Reiki explains that Chiryo means treatment and Heso is the navel area that is the original source of nurturing. It recommends healing on and around the navel at every opportunity since it builds up the immune system.

Hibiki ヒビキ
The feelings or sensations the healer feels when he senses Byosen with the hands.

Higher self ハイヤー・セルフ
Spirit, which is the foundation of a human. It is called in various ways: transcendence self, true self, great self that connects to the Universe, divine self, essential life and so on.

Hikari no Kokyu-ho (Light Breathing) 光の呼吸法
One of the Gendai Reiki Ho's Gihos to restore the resonance with Reiki when negative thoughts and emotions arise. First you take in Reiki as the white Light from the crown to fill the whole body and then expand Reiki out of your body.

Jaki 邪気
The energy that has become negative because of stagnation or other reasons. The energy mixed in with negative Nen, such as hatred or anger.

Kenyoku-ho 乾浴法, Kenyoku (Dry Bathing) 乾浴
Japan has a tradition to bathe before religious rituals for purification. 乾 Ken means dry and 浴 Yoku means bathing. Kenyoku is the Giho to purify body and mind with Reiki energy instead of water.

Koki-ho (blowing) 呼気法
Healing technique to blow Reiki over the untouchable areas, burn injuries and skin sores.

Kokoro .心
Considering that a human is composed of three elements, body, Kokoro (mind) and spirit, the body is like the hardware and Kokoro is like the software, and spirit can be be thought of as the main system to operate them. (In Japanese, the term 'Kokoro' gives broader meanings according to the context, for example, mind, heart, feelings, self, whole, spirit, faith, consciousness, will, personality, idea, philosophy and so on.)

Komyo 光明
Bright light. The Light emanates from Buddha's whole body, representing wisdom and mercy (compassion) of Buddha. 'To get or achieve Komyo' means to reach satori or enlightenment.

Kotodama コトダマ、言霊
The mysterious power that was believed to reside in words. The term of 'kotodama' is used as the same meaning of mantra.

Mantra マントラ
Words that have mysterious power in Buddhist terms. Devotional songs in Veda, holy text of Hinduism.

Nen 念
Strong will, strong desire, emotional force, intention, intense concentration, strong control by mind or consciousness. As Nen tend to be used to satisfy ego or selfish desire, Reiki healers are taught not to use it while healing.

Nentatsu-ho (Sending Message Technique) 念達法
The Giho to affirm the consciousness of Love and Harmony in words. You can practice Nentatsu before giving Reiki healing, similar to a prayer, to convey the purpose of healing to the Universe and healee. Once the healing gets started, the healer must leave everything to Reiki and never uses Nen.

Oku-den Zenki 奥伝前期
Those who have completed 初伝 Sho-den (who are certified as 三等 3rd tou rankers) can go on to Oku-den if they choose to do so. Oku-den is divided into two levels, Oku-den Zenki (the first half) and Oku-den Koki (the second half). In Oku-den Zenki the practitioner receives two symbols that enhance the power and quality of Reiki energy and more advanced healing skills are taught and practiced.

凝視法 Gyoshi-ho was taught, mostly, in Oku-den Zenki but some Shihans taught in Shoden. The Gakkai does not teach it now. The Oku-den practitioner is required to share the benefit of Reiki with as many people as possible. In Usui Sensei's time and to the end of World War II, in both the first and second half of Oku-den, practitioners were required to provide healing sessions for the public. (Note: The Gakkai today offers healing only to member and their families.)

Oku-den Koki (the second half of Oku-den) 奥伝後期
Once Oku-den Zenki is completed the student will be qualified to take Oku-den Koki. In Oku-den Koki, the student is given the third symbol and required to keep practicing distant healing with it. When h/she finishes it, during Shihan-kai, a meeting attended by Shihans only, the students ability and the knowledge they have acquired since they became a student is discussed. When all the Shihans agree about the competence of the student, the Gakkai issues a certificate to certify that the practitioner has completed the whole coure of Usui Reiki Ryoho. Some of those who had completed this training, as an example, the chiefs in branch offices or others who assist the Shihans were also shown how to give reiju and aome were asked to give reiju to students at training sessions. Now in the Gakkai, only the Shihan is allowed to give reiju.

Reiji-ho 霊示法
The technique to let Reiki guide one's hands to Byosen areas. It is described as, 'The hands get called. '

Reiju 霊授
The energy transmission technique handed down from Usui Sensei; the traditional form of the attunement. It opens the pipe of Reiki flow and allows you to heal by hand. The members of Usui Reiki Ryoho Gakkai are expected to attend the study meetings as many times as possible because being given reiju repeatedly is effective to heighten their inner Reiki.

Reiki 霊気
An energy that has been present before the beginning of the Universe and exists everywhere. It harmonizes everything and helps everything heal and evolve. It is life force energy that is guided by the highest level of consciousness in the Universe and is filled with the hado of love. Its purpose is to carry out the will of the highest consciousness and at the same time, it always respects the free will of the individual.

Reiki Ho 霊気法

The term of 霊気療法 Reiki 'Ryoho' was commonly used in Japan before more recent times. Now it indicates that its purpose is only to heal disease because 療法 'ryoho' literally means therapy, medical treatment or remedy. To clearly specify that the practice of Reiki is the system of how to use Reiki energy in order to live a healthy and happy life, Gendai Reiki Ho uses the term of 法 'Ho,' which means method, technique or system.

Reiki Mawashi 霊気回し

In this effective healing circle, people hold hands—left palm up, right palm down—and the Reiki energy circulates through everyone in the circle and heightens the quality of Reiki.

Satori 悟り

To see through the true nature of things, insight. In Buddhism, it means to be one with the Universe by going beyond mind and emotions, which wander ceaselessly. In Gendai Reiki Ho, satori means the complete resonance of the inner Reiki of the person and the Universal Reiki.

Seiyo Reiki (Western Reiki) 西洋レイキ

The Reiki system that was exported abroad through Chujiro Hayashi Sensei and Hawayo Takata Sensei. Being practiced in many countries, it was re-imported back to Japan in 1980s.

Shihan 師範

In Japanese, Shihan generally means 'the instructor who teaches how to do something by showing the right way to do it.' In order to let the Shinpi-den practitioners learn more, Usui Sensei assigned them to some tasks; Shihan was one of them. They could develop themselves by teaching with Usui Sensei's advice. The system has changed since Usui Sensei passed away; now in the Gakkai, the person who is formally nominated as Shihan is automatically given a Shinpi-den title.

Shin-nen Reiju-kai 新年霊授会

Every January, people who were authorized to perform reiju got together in the head office. Usui Sensei talked to them and gave them reiju. Then they exchanged reiju with each other and made an oath for their own spiritual development and to use Reiki to make a contribution. The Gakkai does not have this event now; NPO Gendai Reiki Network organizes it every year.

Shinpi-den 神秘伝
The practical course to achieve Anshin Ritsumei, the final goal of Dento Reiki that was taught by Usui Sensei. Usui Sensei selected those who were spiritually advanced among Oku-den Koki, the practitioners who were certified to have completed the whole course of Usui Reiki Ryoho to take this training. This training included one on one lectures for spiritual advancement. At the same time Usui Sensei assigned them; 1) to instruct the members as Shihan, 2) to run the Gakkai as a board member and 3) to check and add the finishing touch after the Oku-den practitioner's healing treatment. In the Shinpi-den level as taught by Usui Sensei and by the Gakkai there is no additional symbol that is given. After Usui Sensei passed on, the Gakkai have not provided the special lessons on Anshin Ritsumei for students; now they only give the above three responsibilities and the Shinpi-den level is considered to be honorary. In the present Usui Reiki Ryoho Gakkai, once one is a Shinpi-den, it is not considered appropriate to talk about Reiki outside of the Gakkai.

Sho-den 初伝
The first grade of Dento Reiki. They start learning 病腺霊感法 Byosen Reikan-ho and 霊示法 Reiji-ho the day they join the Gakkai; both are the techniques to find Byosen and are the starting point of Dento Reiki. 乾浴 Kenyoku is one part of 発霊法 Hatsurei-ho. This is also taught the first day, as they practice Hatsurei-ho by the guidance of a Shihan. It starts from 六等 the 6th tou (grade/rank). When they become 三等 the 3rd tou, they are certified as they have completed 'the basics of hand healing' and they can go to Oku-den level if they choose to do so. They are considered to have enough ability to give healing session to themselves and family and friends.

Shuyo-kai 修養会
This is the only training workshop held by Usui Reiki Ryoho Gakkai before WWII. They held Shuyo-kai every day in Tokyo head office, about twice a month in local branches. They practiced Hatsurei-ho under Shihan's instruction, received reiju and exercised Hibiki detection, Reiji-ho, hand healing, and so on. Shuyo-kai was called 霊授会 Reiju-kai when there was only one Shihan. After WWII, it is called 研究会 Kenkyu-kai and held three times a month in head office, once a month in branches.

Spiritual Awareness 気づき
To understand intuitively the true meaning of an event. Satori can be reached by entering into spiritual awareness repeatedly.

Tanden Chiryo-ho 丹田治療法
Dento Reiki's detoxification Giho. Tanden is a chakra below the navel. Dento Reiki Tanden as a place three-finger widths below the navel. In Tanden Chiryo-ho Nentatsu acts to accumulate toxins of the whole body in the Tanden, where they are then excreted from.

Teate Ryoho (Hand healing) 手当療法
'Te' means hand or palm in Japanese. The verb 'ate ru' means to put on. The combination of these two words, te and ate means to put hand(s) on something in this context. Teate Ryoho is a healing art mainly accomplished by putting hand(s) on and also holding over as needed.

Usui Reiki Ryoho 臼井霊気療法
Usui Sensei (1865 – 1926) perfected Usui Reiki Ryoho as a system to reach 安心立命 Anshin Ritsumei starting from hands-on healing, the pathway to health and happiness. It's been spreading worldwide as Usui Reiki or Usui shiki (method, system) Reiki.

Usui Reiki Ryoho Gakkai 臼井霊気療法学会
The group that was founded by Usui Sensei in 1922 and has been continuing to practice his teachings and Gihos.

White Light 白い光
Gendai Reiki explains that Reiki is White Light, since white light includes all the wavelengths of all the colored lights. One of the unique natures of Reiki is that it flows to where needed as much as needed allowing things happen when needed. Reiki works comprehensively for any purpose.

Index

***Bold number** means definition*